HEAL YOUR LIFE

HEAL YOUR LIFE

25 Ways to Unleash Your Innate Healing Powers by Finding Your Purpose and Connecting With a Higher Power

CAROLLE JEAN-MURAT, MD

ISBN: 978-1-63161-030-1

Published by TCK Publishing
www.TCKPublishing.com

Get discounts and special deals on books at
www.tckpublishing.com/bookdeals

CONTENTS

PREFACE

———⁓———

I WAS BORN CAROLLE JEAN IN PORT-AU-PRINCE HAITI IN 1950. My father came from a highly educated family of lawyers, judges, and teachers. His father Emanuel was a pharmacist.

On the other hand, my mother's father was renowned voodoo priest and indigenous healer Mirabeau Murat, who we called Grand-Père. None of my family on Mother's side had graduated from primary school.

When I was four years old and my baby sister Marise was two, my parents separated, and Mother, my sister Marise, and I went to live in my Grand-Père's compound known as Lakou Déréal in Bizoton, a small town outside of Port au Prince. But my father wanted us to live with his mother, who we called Grandma, and her daughter Julia, called Tatante, away from the influence of voodoo on my mother's side of the family.

Mother refused to let us go then found herself pregnant with twins and plagued with severe nausea and vomiting, no longer able to work as a seamstress to feed us. There were no social programs to help impoverished women with small children in Haiti.

Grandma finally convinced Mother to let my sister and I live with her and Tatante. They would take care of us and give us an opportunity to get a good education. Mother made the biggest sacrifice a mother could make and agreed to something she never forgave herself for until her death.

Grandma was a devout Catholic and went to church several times a week. She belonged to the Guard of Honor for the Sacred Heart of Jesus, whose members prayed at least an hour each day. My earliest memory of her is of a loving woman seated on a small chair in her back yard, slowly reading a prayer book and singing hymns. Sometimes, she spent even more time praying, and I learned later on that it was her way to cope with life's hardships.

Back when Grandma was thirty-six years old, Father was sixteen, and Tatante fourteen, Grandma told her abusive husband to leave. This was at a time when women were considered a man's property, but Grandma would not tolerate any kind of abuse. She remained single after that and continued to live with Tatante after Father left home at seventeen to fend for himself.

Grandma was a kind, gentle person, a healer in her own right. She had a special paper bag full of many smaller bags, each one filled with a different herb. She knew all the herbs by name and just how much to give you to make you feel better.

Unfortunately, Tatante was an angry, unhappy spinster. She had been seriously ill with a severe upper respiratory tract infection, and she had lost the man of her dreams. She didn't like my mother and despised her relatives in Lakou Déréal because of what she called "bad blood running in their voodoo veins." She was determined that Marise and I were going to have the best education, but in order to do so, we had to stay away from Mother and her family and go to Catholic school. Tatante was extremely strict with us.

The rare times I got to visit my mother's side of the family, Grand-Pere Mirabeau showered me with love and affection, something that was greatly lacking at home because of Tatante. I could not understand why Tatante called him an evil person. People looked up to him with admiration, and many would stop by with fruits, eggs, and baked goods to thank him for saving their lives or helping a family member who had been very sick.

My father was the tallest and most handsome man I had ever seen. He had the most beautiful smile. He was always working but visited us when he could. He was adamant that we had to follow the rules set by Tatante, and I did my best to be a good Catholic girl. At one point, I proudly told Father that I wanted to be a nun, just like my favorite teacher Soeur Yvonne. He hugged me and said, "You can be anything you want to be." He promised to continue to financially support my sister and me the best he could.

I was told over and over at home that I should never mention Grand-Père Mirabeau and his voodoo compound, especially to those at the prestigious parochial school I attended. But when I was eight, my secret was discovered, and throughout the school year, the teachers ostracized me. I was eventually expelled under the pretext that I had been writing dirty notes to a classmate, which wasn't true.

Shocked and deeply hurt that the nuns lied to Grandma when she questioned the reason for expelling me, I became distressed and very ill as a result. I was taken to many doctors who were not able to help me get well. Eventually, my mother was allowed to take me to Lakou Déréal, where Grand-Père restored my health through his indigenous healing powers, after Western medical doctors had given up on me. This made such a great impression that I decided I would become a doctor since I no longer wanted to be a nun.

A few years later, I had an unexpected, shocking incident. I went looking for my girlfriend at her home. Her twenty-two-year-old brother let me in and suddenly pushed me into his room, closing the door behind him. A moment later, I felt excruciating pain between my legs. It moved upward until it consumed my entire body. My mind went blank.

I stumbled home and into the shower. It did nothing to ease the pain, but as the blood ran down my leg I stood under the flowing water, unmoving, feeling violated and filthy, until I heard Grandma's voice telling me to get ready. We were going to church to be part of a street procession. I dried off, winced through the pain to get dress, and followed Grandma.

Walking hurt, and I could hardly keep up. Why did we have to go marching to let Satan know we were there watching when we had one in our own backyard? Where were the warriors of God? Where were God and Jesus when I was being violated? I pressed on, trying not to think about what had happened to me. I vowed not to tell anyone. In most people's eyes, I was dirty enough already because of Mother's voodoo heritage.

I grew up under the wrath of Francois "Papa Doc" Duvalier's dictatorship in Haiti with curfews and violent oppression. The *tontons macoutes* boogeymen were his paramilitary force that kept the country under siege and committed human rights abuses from 1957 until his death in 1971. People were systematically jailed, killed, or just disappeared, like my uncle Charlemagne did when I was ten years old.

One late night when I was 14, there was banging at the front door. In stumbled Father, his face swollen, his arms bruised. The night before while he'd been asleep, a group of tontons macoutes broke into his house and at gunpoint took him outside. They tied his hands behind his back and thrashed him then drove him off toward Fort Dimanche, the dungeon of death, where all political killings take place. Fortunately, a friend of his was there and intervened, so they eventually let him go. But they told him they were going to come back for him and were going to kill him. My father had no choice but to go into exile.

"*Au nom the l'éternel,* nothing will happen to you," Grandma said with great faith. "Jesus and the Virgin Mary have you under their protection, and no *démon, Satan, Je renonce,* can harm you."

He left Haiti. Grandma spent hours and hours praying for Father until we finally received a letter six months later telling us he was safe in Martinique.

That same year, Grand-Père Mirabeau died. Although I loved him very much, Tatante and society made me feel too ashamed to be seen at his funeral, and regretfully, I did not go to the large ceremony held for him at a Masonic Temple.

I dutifully went to confession on Saturday afternoons and would attend the 8:00 a.m. Mass on Sundays. I also joined the church choir because I loved to sing. Choir practice took place on Saturday afternoons. I went to confession after every practice.

I was fifteen years old when I saw a neighbor, a well-known tonton macoute, at church. He was kneeling at the confessional pew. I was enraged. Books were rare to come by, but I found one explaining about the Inquisition in Spain and how confessions were used to arrest and kill defiant people. I resented that the tontons macoutes could kill people and then go to confession and beg for forgiveness.

One Saturday night, I was lamenting I didn't have a decent dress to wear to mass in the morning. Money was tight. Grandma decided it would be better if we went to the 4:00 a.m. Mass instead of the one at eight. Then I realized that the people who attended very early Mass were the poor who didn't have decent clothing to wear and had to do their worshiping in the dark, where no one could see them. I told Grandma and Tatante I did not want to go to a place with such discrimination. I also told them I didn't want to go to confession, either, because I did not consider myself a sinner who needed to repent for her sins. What sins? I was not like the tontons macoutes, who threatened, harassed, and killed people for no reason. I stopped going to confession.

Then Papa Doc Duvalier decided he wanted only black, Haitian priests in Haiti. Rumors were that most were tontons macoutes who wore guns under their robes. All the white priests left the country.

That was when I found the courage to tell Tatante and Grandma that I would no longer go to church, and there was nothing they could do about it. They were shocked!

I never did go back to church. Every Sunday morning after Mass, Tatante and Grandma would kiss me and say, "We pray that the devil in you will one day leave you." They would say nothing else to me on those mornings.

I was athletic in and out of school and played volleyball well enough to make the Olympic team. But when it was time to show my passport to compete in the 1968 Olympic Games, I was too ashamed to show my birth certificate with my mother's maiden name Murat. I declined to go, another deep regret, because of my mother's family connection to the voodoo religion.

Father eventually ended up working in New York and encouraged me to join him. When I left Haiti in 1970 bound for the United States, I was twenty years old and had big dreams. I hoped to be accepted into medical school at a French-speaking university in Europe. I was determined to return to Haiti as a doctor to help the poor people.

Papa Doc Duvalier died peacefully in his sleep. He had committed so many horrendous crimes, and the thought appalled me that he could just ask for forgiveness before his death, and, according to the church, he'd go to Heaven.

That was when I decided there was no God.

When I arrived in the United States with my sisters Marise and Fifi, my plan was to stay in Brooklyn for only a few months. I did not have the opportunity to go to medical school in Europe as I had planned but ended up two years later with my friend Nicole at the Autonomous University of Guadalajara School of Medicine in Mexico. I started on August 4, 1972. When all the paperwork was done, the secretary handed me my ID card. It read Carolle Jean-Murat.

I learned that in Mexico it was the custom to carry the father's and the mother's last names. I looked at the card and at the last name I had been ashamed of all my life. The name I feared so much that I had missed one of the greatest opportunities as an athlete—to participate in the Olympics. I then remembered what Grand-Père told me—*never forget where you came from*—and I made a decision. From then on, I would carry the Murat name with pride.

To be accepted into a postgraduate program in the U.S. as we planned, we needed to spend a year interning at an accredited hospital and another year of Servicio Social—Social Services—with the Department of Public Health in Mexico. At the end of that year, I took the final exam and obtained my Physician and Surgeons diploma, the *Titulo de Medico Cirujano*. Meanwhile, I still had to pass the ECFMG exam given by the Educational Council for Foreign Medical Graduates in order to be accepted into a residency program in the U.S.

Nicole and another friend, Jocelyne, ended up at the University of the West Indies in Jamaica in July 1976. I was lucky to be trained by nurse midwives in Jamaica in a very busy hospital, where I had the opportunity to become an experienced surgeon, something that would come in handy during my residency training in Milwaukee.

Grandma came to spend three months with me in Montego Bay. It was my first opportunity to give back something to her for all the sacrifices she had made for her favorite granddaughter.

She was very sad to learn I still did not believe in God. She reiterated how important it was to have God in my life. But she was my "spiritual link." I started the habit of telling her about the tough cases I encountered during my training. She would ask me the names of the patients and spend time praying especially for them. I appreciated her praying for someone she didn't even know. She would always remind me that prayers work! I started to notice that those she prayed for would get well when everyone was expecting them to die. I called her my "prayer warrior."

Returning to rural Mexico in July 1977, I spent a year in community medicine. I delivered babies, often without running water or electricity. I was then accepted for postgraduate training in obstetrics and gynecology at Mount Sinai Medical Center in Milwaukee, Wisconsin, where I nearly froze to death! I married one of my fellow residents, who was doing his training in internal medicine, and we decided to move to San Diego. Unfortunately, I found out the day before I took my written exam in order to become board-certified, that my husband was having an affair. He said he would end it. I was devastated but had to try to put the hurt aside to concentrate on my medical career.

I called Grandma, who was living in New York with Father, to tell her about my predicament and about my fear that I would not be able to take the exam. She told me not to worry; she was going to light a candle and pray during the time of the exam. Grandma asked me to join her in her favorite song—*Oh saint esprit donnez-nous vos lumières, venez en nous pour nous embrasser tous. Guidez no pas et formez nos prières, nous ne pouvons faire aucun bien sans vous. Oh, Holy Spirit, give us your lights, come to us to embrace us all. Guide us in our prayers, we cannot do any good without you.* Grandma was always so strong, and her faith was unwavering. I never had that kind of strength or faith, but she had enough for both of us, and I did pass the exam...with flying colors.

The last two months of my training were spent at UCLA. By then, I was licensed to practice medicine in Wisconsin and had earned reciprocity to practice in California. I had also passed the written board for my specialty. Two years later, after passing my oral board examination, I became a board-certified obstetrician and gynecologist, and eventually, a Fellow of the American College of Obstetricians and Gynecologists.

I was planning to open a private practice in November 1982 with my husband who trained as an internist. But I found out that his affair had continued, and he had even brought the woman to sleep in my bed while I was at UCLA. I told him to leave and called Grandma, sick and sobbing about what had happened, asking her to come and help me.

The next day, I was at the airport, picking her up. Grandma brought along a homemade remedy based on castor oil and Haitian *lamidon*, a white starchy powder, to make a porridge that helped soothe my aching stomach. For the first two days, while praying, she spoon-fed me and rubbed my stomach with the oil. I soon felt better under grandma's loving care.

I knew San Diego would be my home. I didn't care that there were few black doctors and not one other black female OB-GYN. I've never minded breaking the ice. For four years, I remained the only female OB-GYN in the hospital where I worked. For twelve years, I was the only black female OB-GYN in private practice.

God was the only thing Grandma and I did not agree on. I knew how important going to church was to her, so during the two years she stayed with me, I made sure she went to Mass every Sunday and midnight Mass on Christmas and Easter. The first few months, I attended church with her but felt it was a waste of time, so I told her I would drop her off and pick her up. After each Mass, she would kiss me on the cheek to give me her blessing, kissing me again on the other cheek to "give me blessings from God." She said she was worried I would not make it to heaven. Jokingly, I told her that when it was time for me to come to the pearly gates, St. Peter would let me in just because I was so good to *her*. We both laughed heartily.

Grandma was my pillar during those days, showing me how prayer could be very effective for my patients. Again, when I had a tough case, I would discuss it with her, and she would take the patient's or the newborn, premature baby's name and pray until everything was resolved. She also taught me how to forgive my ex-husband through prayer, which, eventually, I did.

Two years later, at the age of eighty, Grandma decided to leave and go stay with my sister Marise, who was pregnant and at risk for going into premature labor. Her doctor had ordered her to stay on bed rest, and she needed help taking care of her one-year-old daughter. Before Grandma left, she told me she was sad that I did not have a close relationship with God. She wanted me to try to believe that I could always find strength in prayers in times of need.

As Grandma held my face in her hands before she left, she said, "Remember that even Jesus could be weak and had to depend on Simon de Cyrene to help him carry the cross at Calvary. So never hesitate to ask for help. You never have to bear your cross alone; please remember that."

I wished I had Grandma's faith. "I will try," I said.

In obstetrics and gynecology, so often things fall into a gray zone. Do you send a pregnant patient home, or does she need to be admitted for observation? Should you operate right away? Will the patient deliver vaginally if given enough time? Is the fetal distress bad enough to warrant a C-section? Does a young woman need a drastic surgery that will render her sterile, or should I wait? Practicing medicine requires using a sixth sense, where clinical knowledge and what's happening to a particular patient merge to help you make the right decisions. Unfortunately, one cannot play God. There is risk of a patient dying and the threat of a malpractice litigation always hanging over a doctor's head.

But I never had to fear listening to my intuitive voice. When I had discussed difficult cases with Grandma, she would tell me to trust that voice, that it was guided by God. I got more and more confident, listening to my inner voice, even when my instincts contradicted scientific knowledge. But all those patients did well.

In 1988, Grandma moved in with Mother, who was living in Miami. The last time I saw Grandma, in January 1991, a few months before her death, once again, she cupped my face with her hands and looked me straight in the eyes. She again emphasized that I would benefit myself and my patients if I developed a strong connection with God.

"But you are here to pray for me and my patients," I told her, trying to make her laugh.

"I will not be always around," she lamented. She died several months later at 87 years old.

As I watched her coffin being lowered into the ground, I felt that a part of me had died. Before I left, Mother handed me a bag containing Grandma's prayer books and rosary that, to our horror, we had forgotten to put in her hands before closing the casket, as was our custom in Haiti.

So I now had Grandma's well-worn, olivewood rosary, which had an amazing history. Reflecting on her unwavering strength of faith as I held it, I remembered Grandma had once prayed for a patient of mine who wanted to have a baby but was unsuccessful after years of effort.

A month later, the couple was pregnant. The husband was to travel to Israel and asked what he could bring my Grandma in appreciation for her prayers. Her only wish was to own a rosary made of olivewood from the Mount of Olives in Israel. He found a beautiful, hand-carved, olivewood rosary and bought it for her, although he probably received surprised looks. Not many Jewish men purchase rosaries.

That was when I realized I'd had so much faith in Grandma's prayers as my backup, that I had been able to trust myself during challenging cases and do what I felt I was supposed to do even when it didn't always make scientific sense. She had enabled me to develop skills that only come when you are born and raised with healers in a poor country. Now that I didn't have her backup, who was going to pray for my patients who needed prayers?

The day after Grandma died, I met Bibi Denise, a powerful, Afrocentric counselor/therapist, who became my mentor regarding the mind-body connection of disease. She suggested I ask my patients who were having extreme PMS, gynecological problems such as irregular bleeding, pelvic pain, or who'd had a hysterectomy or any female organs removed, if they had experienced sexual abuse in the past. There was a very apparent connection, and the issue came up again when I became a provider for the VA, treating female soldiers or veterans and started to learn about military sexual trauma, or MST.

Discovering that so many of my patients had been molested or sexually abused as children, teenagers, or as adults—often by someone close to them—was a real eye-opener. I became the confidante to many who felt they could reveal these awful secrets, which they had—to their bodies' detriment—suppressed for years.

And I finally understood why I was plagued with PMS, pelvic pain, and had horrible menstrual periods.

For many years, I took time with my patients in labor, and my C-section rate was about half of those of my colleagues. I always felt confident about my decision to hold off. But when Grandma died, I no longer had that trust since I didn't have her powerful prayer to back me up.

In January 1992, five months after Grandma's death, I was asked to perform a C-section. Fearing I might be sued if I waited and the baby was born with damage, I went against my better judgment and performed the operation. I became nauseous after the procedure, and when I got home, I threw up violently. I decided then and there to quit delivering babies. How could I ever know in the future if a patient really needed a C-section, or if I'd allowed my fear to take over? I decided to continue with my gynecological practice only. I was forty-two years old.

At this time, managed care became a stronger force, dictating how to practice medicine, how little time to spend with patients, and how much I would be paid, while I had no voice on how much I was required to pay for malpractice insurance.

I struggled to spend adequate time with my patients, listening to them about their familiar symptoms and past traumatic issues, often referring them to counseling to help them further understand and resolve their gynecological problems. I was treating the whole human being, not just symptoms. Surgical interventions started to diminish as I was able to heal more patients without a knife!

In 1997, I met esteemed author and spiritual healer Louise Hay at a conference, and soon thereafter, she became my friend and patient. I had started to write books, and in 1999, her Hay House Publishing Company published my award-winning book *Menopause Made Easy: How to Make the Right Decisions for the Rest of Your Life.* Ms. Hay wrote an important chapter for that book called "Healthy Aging." My book *Natural Pregnancy A-Z* was published the following year.

Due to rising malpractice costs, I performed my last operation in June 1999. However, I was in the prime of my career as a forty-eight-year-old gynecological surgeon, and my intention was to continue seeing and counseling patients, doing only minor office surgeries, plus find ways to do volunteer medical work.

I decided to join Dr. Charles Rene, a fellow OB-GYN from Haiti who practiced in Louisiana. He and his team went several times a year to the poorer sections of Haiti, and I decided this would be a great way to put my surgical skills to good use. While I was preparing for the trip, Mother became ill and died in September; she was only seventy years old. One month later, Guy, my sister Fifi's husband, was involved in a horrible car accident and sustained third-degree burns over half his body. When I landed in Haiti, I learned he was comatose and not expected to live. My emotions were in turmoil.

In Haiti, I found myself working in a small, extremely primitive hospital. There was no running water or electricity. The medical challenges were so severe that, in addition to performing surgeries, I struggled to create community programs to provide health education and scholarships for the children.

All this emotional upheaval and stress built up and brought on frightening, unexpected panic attacks. The first one occurred while I was on a tour to promote my books in New York City. I turned to Bibi Denise as my therapist. Since I couldn't sleep, she suggested I see my doctor and temporarily be placed on an anti-anxiety medication and a sleeping pill.

I couldn't understand what was going on with me. Bibi Denise tried to explain my situation. According to her, we as human beings are comprised of the mind, body, and spirit. When we stray from the spiritual beliefs of our ancestors, we suffer the most.

I was the perfect example. Although raised in the Catholic religion with Grandma who had unwavering faith, I had turned my back on religion and, due to the sexual abuse I endured, the Catholic nuns' condemnation of my mother's family, and the atrocities I experienced while living in a war zone in my country, I had decided *there was no God*. Instead, I chose science to explain my existence.

I developed a love-hate relationship with those bottles of medication. The pills helped with anxiety and allowed me to sleep, but they also made me dizzy and unfocused. I could not concentrate and was constantly on the edge of losing my balance.

Denise saw my distress and gently suggested I try something else—to work through Grandma, the person I trusted most and with whom I had the strongest spiritual connection. Eventually, I could go directly to God without an intermediary, but for now, my strong connection with Grandma was all I had.

I decided to try, using Grandma's olivewood rosary to help me feel close to her. I sat on my bed with the rosary in my hands and cried. I read through her prayer book. I visualized her sitting in her favorite chair in our backyard in Haiti, reading from this book.

"Grandma, I don't like the way I am feeling; please, come to help me," I begged.

I saw her smiling at me. What did she say when she'd endured tough times? When there was not enough food to feed us? When my father had financial and political troubles and our shoes were worn out? The answer came to me then: *"Jésus, doux Jésus, mon maître et mon sauveur; vrais pain des forts, soutenez-moi je suis si faible...* Jesus, sweet Jesus, my master and my savior, the Lord of the strong, help me I am weak..."

I fell asleep while repeating the prayer over and over as I clutched Grandma's rosary. When I awoke, it was morning, and the sun was high in the sky. I felt rested, but more importantly, I realized a spiritual healing had occurred that night for me. Everything had changed. I felt better, stronger. I withdrew from the medications, was able to sleep, and felt balanced and focused again.

I learned about the power of forgiveness during therapy and felt guided to make peace with Tatante, who had passed away a year later. I had found the strength to make big changes in my life.

I continued to help my people in Haiti, but I quit private practice in California completely. Then came an opportunity to open the first wellness center in the country in 2003, as my gifts as an intuitive healer became stronger.

I turned my home in Mt. Helix, San Diego, into a retreat center. Those who were ready would come and spend time with me to discover and heal the "root cause" of their symptoms, which remained unresolved by prescription-writing, American doctors. When time permitted, I also conducted daylong seminars and retreats. Some people came to me from as far away as England for "root-cause healing" of persistent physical and emotional symptoms.

Father had always supported me in whatever decisions I made regarding my medical career. When I explained to him how I was now able to help patients, he reminded me I was a "divine mirror" who helped them see who they really were, who helped them connect their past to their present conditions, which allowed them to take charge of their lives and to heal.

A devastating earthquake hit my beloved Haiti on January 12, 2010. Every landmark I knew—the churches, including the National Cathedral, the schools I had attended, city buildings, such as the White House, the homes I built for poor relatives in Lakou Déréal—all were destroyed. In La Vallée, a portion of the hospital collapsed. Half the homes were badly damaged and another third completely destroyed.

I went to Haiti to help in any way I could. Since there were no medical supplies available and there were so many patients to attend to, and knowing that they had a strong faith in God, I started to pray with them and was gratified when so many improved or were completely healed.

When I spoke to Reverend Destinace Vilsaint, a member of the Haitian Society of San Diego, about how patients would improve and heal when I prayed with them, he explained that I did an "intercession" while holding their hands, and then I had a "revelation" that let me know what I was supposed to do or say. I then gave my patients the opportunity to manifest their faith, enabling them to heal themselves.

"You are just the conduit, Dr. Carolle," he said.

As I returned again and again to Haiti, my reputation grew as the spiritual healer who would heal through prayers. I was amazed at the faith people professed in the middle of such chaos and loss, and how they were able to heal and go on with their lives. I wished I had that kind of faith for myself.

Then in November 2014, after a grueling two weeks spent working at our small hospital, I noticed a picture of Jesus the Sacred Heart with a halo above his head and his hand extended. It was the Sacred Heart! The one Grandma and my patients prayed to.

That night, after a very long day at the hospital, I lay down in my bed, and my stomach started to hurt. As I became weaker and weaker after so many trips to the bathroom with diarrhea and vomiting, the image of Jesus the Sacred Heart I had seen earlier came to mind. Then I heard a soft voice whispering in my ear. "You have used me for so many years to heal your patients. Why don't you ask me to help you?"

But how could I, I wondered? I did not have their faith. All of a sudden, I could feel the presence of my ancestors—Grand-Père Mirabeau, Grandma, Mother, Father, even Tatante— all cheering me on.

"Yes, you can do it. It is now the time to surrender, to be able to appreciate the peace we all have experienced with our faith. Just trust, say the words, and you will be healed and be free forever," they whispered in unison.

With their strength surrounding me and allowing me to get out of my scientific mind, I took a leap of faith. As I have taught my patients with IBS, ulcerative colitis, and other gastrointestinal disturbances to ease their discomfort, I put both hands over the area that was painful on my body and took slow, deep breaths. I repeated over and over, "Jesus, I have faith in you; please, help me!"

The next thing I knew, I was awakened by the cry of a rooster. The sun was up. I had slept for nine straight hours. There was no nausea, no feeling of having to throw up, no loose bowels, no more pain. The brighter the day became, the stronger I felt.

A miracle had occurred; I had relied on faith and was physically healed. I felt strong, ready to tackle my last day at the hospital in Haiti and return home to the busy primary care clinic I was working at part-time in San Diego. I felt I had a stronger power to aid my patients in healing.

When Mary, a fifty-two-year-old woman, came into the clinic in San Diego, I looked at her chart and saw all the illnesses plaguing her, all the medications she was taking—and all the side effects of those medications—and that she was still suffering. I could see her spirit was crumbling with the weight of life.

"Mary, what has been happening to you?" I asked her.

"It all started when my husband passed away five years ago. He died of a heart attack in my arms. Since then, my health has been slowly deteriorating."

I extended my hands to her, and she held them.

"I'm tired, Doctor, I am tired," she said as she held on to me tightly, tears running down her cheeks.

"Do you have faith in a higher power; do you pray?" I asked her.

"I'm a Christian, but I have not prayed or gone to church lately. I'm so overwhelmed."

Just as with all the other patients I'd encountered whose diseases were progressing, instead of reviving her faith during a time of bad health and loss, Mary turned away from it. Many of my former patients had even become mad at God, asking, "Why me?" instead of realizing they should strengthen their faith, so they could find solace and the ability to heal themselves.

As I held Mary's hands and prayed with her, I could feel the energy coming down from the heavens and through my head, through my heart, into my hands, and then out to Mary, filling her up with it just like a deflated balloon filling up with air.

We prayed, and I watched her posture straighten, her eyes become brighter. I could not help but smile.

That was when I fully realized *my* faith had been restored; that I was now a true spiritual healer, just like Grandma and Grand-Père. I could use my medical and scientific knowledge along with the power of faith to help my patients on a much deeper level.

"The antidote to chaos is Faith."

"Faith will Light the Darkened Sky."

"Faith is the Essence of All Things"

"Faith within a belief system, religious or not, that is all powerful, merciful, forgiving, understanding, can only strengthen your relationship with God."

"Faith often involves persistence and patience."

"Faith is confidence that you will receive what you desire before you actually have it."

"Faith involves a kind of positive thinking that by itself heals and prepares the body for healing."

"Faith is not belief without proof or belief despite the evidence; rather, faith is a complete trust or confidence in someone or something. That trust or confidence we have in someone is built up over time as he proves himself faithful time and time again."

"He who loses money, loses much; He who loses a friend, loses much more; He who loses faith, loses all."

Eleanor Roosevelt

"Faith is a confidant belief in a supreme being, which most call God, an accessible and lovable being who listens to prayers and responds."

"For the chronically ill, the search for physical healing can often become an unobtainable idol in their lives. Faith can put that physical illness beneath us, where it belongs, return dominion to us and give us power to live victorious and fulfilled lives."

"Faith is the breakfast of champions. It is the staple diet of those fearless enough to see the invisible, hear the inaudible, and attempt the impossible."

"Faith alone will carry you through when intellect and emotion are depleted."

Iyanla Vanzant

INTRODUCTION

WE MAY NOT REALIZE IT AT FIRST, BUT WE ARE ALL ON A spiritual journey.

My hope is that by using the suggestions and examples in this book, you will be able to develop your own personal spiritual practices to strengthen your faith, so you will have help when you are faced with difficult challenges, pain, and trauma.

Faith means many things to many people. To me, faith means believing in something greater than myself that can be there for me 24/7.

According to opinion polls, the vast majority of Americans still believe in God or a higher power. But there are strong signs that many are less certain about this belief than in years past. Many were raised in a religious family, suffered from trauma and abuse as a child or adult, and decided there was no God—*just like I did.*

In my experience, people who were raised in a family with no spiritual connections or who went astray as I did from the spiritual beliefs of their childhood are more likely to be plagued with emotional and physical symptoms later on. And there are those who lose faith when something bad happens to them or to a loved one, and they become angry with God.

Many studies have shown that those with faith in God or a higher power will use it to help overcome the hardships of emotional and physical illness and to improve their quality of life and well-being. They are more likely to triumph over heartbreaking separation, loss, grief, pain, chronic disease, anxiety, depression, etc.

My life story, a portion of which I shared in the preface, has been compiled into a book called *True Healing Through Faith*, and there are plans to make it into a feature film. But when I finished the manuscript, I felt that something was missing. Yes, it's an inspiring story, but how could I be more helpful to those who find themselves in the same situation that I experienced?

The answer came as an inspiration to write *this book*—to help those whose faith is lacking, to help rekindle it, so they can use that power to live a healthier and more peaceful life.

In the following pages, you will find twenty-five ways that many of my patients and I learned to help solidify and call on our faith, especially during hard times.

You can read through each one, or answer the "Your Faith Inventory" questions, and go directly to those you feel inspired to work on. At the end of each short chapter are questions to answer about the subject and a place to create steps to harness the power of faith for yourself.

Do these steps at your own pace, and don't worry if you only make a little progress at a time. Finding or regaining your faith in a higher power does not usually come about overnight. It can start gradually, and then, all of a sudden you realize, as I did, that it's there, *and that it works...*

To your health in faith and love,

Dr. Carolle

YOUR FAITH INVENTORY

I don't know my reason(s) for living.	YES / NO
I don't know my life purpose.	YES / NO
I feel I have no choices.	YES / NO
I don't have healthy boundaries in my relationships. For instance, I don't know how to say no, or I allow others to monopolize my time.	YES / NO
I'm dealing with disappointments or betrayals.	YES / NO
I'm plagued with worries.	YES / NO
I'm filled with regrets.	YES / NO
I have past issues of abuse.	YES / NO
I don't know how to take it one day at a time.	YES / NO
I don't know how to listen to my intuition.	YES / NO
I'm not dealing with stress well.	YES / NO
I don't know how to "be in the moment."	YES / NO
There are people I need to forgive.	YES / NO
I don't use affirmations.	YES / NO
I have difficulty shedding tears.	YES / NO
I don't know how to ask for help.	YES / NO
I need to learn about true friendship.	YES / NO
I'd like to learn how giving can increase my faith.	YES / NO
I don't have a list of things for which I am grateful.	YES / NO

I have difficulty keeping faith through adversities.	YES / NO
There are no people in my life who truly walk in faith.	YES / NO
I'd like to learn how reading can increase my faith.	YES / NO
I don't pray.	YES / NO
I have difficulty surrendering.	YES / NO
I am not part of a spiritual or religious community.	YES / NO

1

FINDING YOUR REASON TO LIVE

HAVING A REASON TO LIVE IS *POWERFUL.* IT WILL GET YOU UP IN the morning; give you motivation to accomplish things in this chaotic world, help you make it through difficult financial situations, health issues, and relationship problems. It goes hand-in-hand with having faith in yourself and faith in a higher power.

Being a healer is my reason for living, but I've questioned it many times over the years.

I had difficulties right from the very beginning—going through medical training in Mexico, Jamaica, and the U.S., being educated in French and needing to study science in Spanish and English, separation from loved ones, and other sacrifices…none of these things were easy…

I remember one day during my residency training in freezing Milwaukee. I was a third-year resident when I came down with the flu. I was on call the night before and had been working non-stop for thirty hours. After helping with a hysterectomy, I felt too tired to walk to the cafeteria to eat, so I went straight to the call room and collapsed. Then my pager buzzed. The number was the busy GYN clinic, where I was supposed to see patients the rest of the afternoon. I ignored the alert, but they paged me again. I decided to call my chief resident who I knew had no other assignments and ask if he could please go to the clinic for me.

He refused, saying I knew when I joined the residency program it wasn't going to be a piece of cake. And then he hung up on me. I didn't know what to do or where I'd find the strength to continue. Maybe I was not suited for this hard work, after all. How dare I think I could aspire to so much and get away with it? My pager continued to go off. Maybe it was time to quit.

Rising through my despair came the image I often used during hard times—a picture of the future me in my white coat, holding in my arms a little girl I had just delivered in my private practice. I saw myself taking pictures with all the other children I had delivered, plastering my office walls with them. Reminded of my reason to live, I called the clinic and told them I was on my way.

"I can't quit; I've come too far, made too many sacrifices, too many people are praying for me, counting on me to succeed, as a Haitian, as a black woman..." Talking to myself out loud, I convinced my battered body to get up, splashed cold water on my face, and headed for the elevator.

The diagnosis of cancer or any life-threatening disease can be a monumental, pivotal moment for anyone. Such an event affects not just the individual, but also their family and friends. Having a reason to live proved to be beneficial to my patients who have survived cancer.

One of these patients was Barbara. She was the caregiver of her six-year-old grandson, and when she was diagnosed with breast cancer, she said she had no time for such "nonsense," as she put it. I helped her picture herself hanging around until he grew up, had a good job, and was able to take care of himself. She lived to see all those things happen.

My sister Fifi was diagnosed with advanced-stage metastatic breast cancer. She went into remission, but the cancer returned fourteen years later in her lungs and around her heart. We were told her case was dire, and she would have to go through chemotherapy and radiation therapy, but there was little chance of the treatments making a difference. However, Fifi was adamant that she wanted to live, so one day she could have the joy of holding a granddaughter in her arms. At that point in their lives, her children were not planning to marry or have babies anytime soon.

While on oxygen, she made her bucket list, which included visiting the new World Trade Center in NYC and going to Dubai to see the Miracle Garden, and she bought her plane tickets a year in advance. She also had the unwavering faith that God was going to heal her. As she suffered through her prescribed treatments, she kept those images in mind. A year later, her doctors could not believe she was cancer-free. The days I received pictures of her beautiful self with New York and Dubai in the background were some of the best moments of my life.

My sixty-five-year-old patient Gina, who had ovarian cancer spread all over her abdomen, longed to be in the delivery room when her daughter or son would have their first baby. This became her reason for living.

I operated on her in 1996. Four years later, in 2000, I called to wish her Happy New Year. She was not at home but in San Francisco at her son's house, visiting with her newborn granddaughter. She said she was now waiting for her daughter to get married and have a baby.

My patient Joyce was having difficulty controlling her diabetes. She was going through many stressors in her life—divorce, unemployment, taking care of her mother with Alzheimer's.

She was able to turn things around when I showed her how to visualize herself in the future, walking—not riding in a wheelchair with her legs amputated—attending the graduation of her granddaughter Julie from San Diego State University. At the time, Julie was only eight years old, but I had Joyce imagine Julie as an adult, throwing her cap into the air. This gave Joyce a reason to live, and whenever she would feel stress, which caused her blood sugar to become out of whack, she would summon this image to calm herself.

Six months later, her blood sugar reverted back to normal. As we worked together, she learned that trusting she was going to get better was also a healing act of faith.

As my mother lay dying years ago, she told me she had no fear, knowing that I would be there for my five grown siblings. I have a close relationship with them, and we share a strong bond of unconditional love. To "mother" other people is another of my reasons to live. I'm known as the family jokester, always ready to make them laugh, regardless of how bad the situation is.

I don't have any children of my own, but there are many people who adopted me as their mom and who are intricate parts of my life. They bring me joy with their presence, and I enjoy being of support to them in their time of need. I joke that I like the idea that we share a deep love, but I didn't have to go through pregnancy and labor, stay awake all night breastfeeding, burp them, and change their diapers!

I also support several children in Haiti through scholarships and community programs. So much was lost during the devastating 2010 earthquake, and I continue to seek funds to retrofit the only trade school in the community of La Vallée de Jacmel to give them the possibility of a better future. I want to continue as long as I live to make a difference in their lives. They, too, are my reasons for living.

MY TRUE HEALING ACTION PLAN

What is my reason to live?

If I don't know my reason(s) for living today, what steps will I take to figure it out? (For example, you can ask yourself who or what might be affected most if you were no longer here. Or perhaps you have a certain cause or charity you are passionate about.)

2

KNOW YOUR LIFE PURPOSE

THE MAJORITY OF MY PATIENTS PLAGUED WITH EMOTIONAL AND physical symptoms are busy dealing with the demands of work, being a spouse, mother, father, or caregiver. They have no clue why they are here on Earth and don't know anything about their life's purpose because they're very focused on daily responsibilities and challenges.

Our life purpose relates to the overall reason we feel we are here in the world. It is about knowing the greater reason behind being alive.

Not knowing your life purpose is like being a small boat lost in the middle of the sea, going nowhere. Not having a port to sail to and without a final destination, when the rough waves of storms hit the boat, it's difficult or impossible to keep sailing.

Having no purpose makes life meaningless and often creates a feeling of not belonging.

Finding your life purpose and believing that who you are and what you do makes a difference in the world will help you heal and thrive in mind, body, and spirit.

I always knew I wanted to be a doctor. I was trained as an OB-GYN, a surgeon who could heal with a knife, but I was transformed into an intuitive and spiritual healer who could heal without a knife. Because of my life's journey and education, I am able to find the root cause of a patient's condition and help those who have suffered for years and wasted time, energy, and money while their health deteriorated.

Being able to show them how the root cause correlates to their present condition and giving them the tools they need to deal with it, is a priceless skill. Knowing that all the obstacles I had to overcome were only the lessons I had to learn to become who I am today not only makes me understand who I really am, it also makes my journey easy and worry-free.

Even better, with the strong faith I have now, knowing I will be taken care of, no matter what, I am able to share this gift with others.

MY TRUE HEALING ACTION PLAN

What is my life purpose?

If my life purpose isn't clear today, what steps will I take to understand it?

3

YOU HAVE CHOICES!

———

I HAVE KNOWN MANY PEOPLE LIVING IN ABUSIVE SITUATIONS who felt helpless because they thought they had no choice and no way out. It may be difficult to assert ourselves and to choose what's good for us, but we can do it if we realize we *do* have choices.

If you believe you don't have any choice, then someone else will make choices for you. The only things you cannot choose are the country of your birth, your parents, your gender, race, and, to a point, your physical appearance. Anything else that happens to you is by your choice, whether conscious or unconscious.

Often, when we feel helpless and out of control, we try to change the status quo. This usually brings us more stress because we worry about making a wrong decision.

I, too, have found myself in situations where I experienced my stress as mental and physical pain. If I dared to think about getting out of the situation I was in, I experienced anxiety.

Many of us do not change because we don't feel strong enough to tackle the job. I have seen many patients who feel "stuck."

But there is always a way out of any situation. We only need to be conscious that we don't like where we are and want to change. So when you find yourself feeling as if there is no way out, make the time to find out why you are in this particular situation, use your clever mind to figure out how to get out of it, and then take action.

Please stop banging your head against the wall or knocking on a door that won't open. Take time to think and look around, as there are always other alternatives.

Don't stay in abusive, intimate relationships for the security of money or a home, especially if you have children. The long-term consequences you and they will suffer are irreversible.

Don't stay in a dead-end or stressful job. I've seen so many patients, including my sister, whose fear of leaving a job with insurance and benefits had them ignore body distress signals, resulting in chronic disease or cancer. Make a Plan B, where you work on other options, such as educating yourself for a promotion or a career change. Those who do this often end up in their dream job. Even though the pay can be less, peace of mind and better health is priceless.

Having faith in a higher power allows you to feel you will be taken care of, no matter what.

MY TRUE HEALING ACTION PLAN

What situation in my life needs to change?

What different choices can I make to change my situation?

4

Setting Healthy Boundaries in Relationships

———~~———

THE WORD "BOUNDARY" IS DEFINED AS "AN INDICATED BORDER or limit." Adults with healthy boundaries have developed an identity distinct from others and know their acceptable limits regarding their responsibility to nurture someone else's personal and spiritual growth.

Having healthy boundaries in any kind of relationship involves both people feeling they are independent beings but close enough to impact each other. In healthy relationships, boundaries remain flexible, but for the most part, each other's needs are met without intimidation or guilt.

Compelling evidence indicates that both men and women experience substantial benefits from having fulfilling relationships with their intimate partners, parents, children, grandchildren, in-laws, extended family, friends, neighbors, and colleagues. They live longer, healthier, wealthier, and happier lives as a result. Our ability to nurture and enjoy such relationships can benefit us mentally, physically, and spiritually.

On the other hand, feeling stuck in a bad or unhealthy relationship will bring on stress. Negative stress occurs when you feel a lack of control over a particular situation.

Not coping well with stress will cause you to be overburdened. Signs of being overburdened are anger, anxiety, denial, depression, exhaustion, health problems, irritability, lack of concentration, insomnia, stomach upset, and social withdrawal.

In order to take control of your life, you will need to create healthy boundaries, and from now on, do things because you *want* to, not just because you *have* to.

How to Set Healthy Boundaries

In order to create healthy boundaries, you need to have a good sense of self and what it is you truly need and want from each relationship. Part of this self-awareness step is figuring out healthy mental, emotional, and physical limits for yourself.

Many people, especially women, do not even know what personal healthy boundaries are and therefore don't know when theirs are being invaded. This is usually true for those raised by abusive caregivers, and also for those who grew up in cultures where women are considered second-class citizens, or for those who had caregivers who themselves had unhealthy boundaries. Those raised in dysfunctional environments will develop survival skills that will translate into adult behaviors that may need adjusting.

If you have issues with self-esteem and are still dealing with scars from childhood abuse, you will need to heal those wounds. It may take some time, but it can be done.

A good step is to take an inventory of all the important relationships in your life, and then ask yourself two questions: Are you being treated with respect, and are your needs are being met? Be honest.

Define each significant relationship in your life, such as intimate partners, relatives, work/career, friends, community, etc. Write down the positive and the negative aspects, what you feel you need in that relationship, and what should be changed.

In many instances, especially involving relatives, the relationship will be very complex. While you are trying to improve yourself, you're surrounded with people you may have chosen unconsciously to help identify and heal your wounds. Sometimes, we may need to walk away from certain relationships, and doing so can be painful.

Working with a counselor as I did, alone or with the other person in your relationship, can be extremely helpful.

Learning and using good communication skills is a must in order to express your needs, establish your boundaries, and to be able to speak up when others are not treating you in an acceptable way.

Setting healthy boundaries with a myriad of relationships is a lifelong process of learning and growth. But it is very important to be able to set and keep healthy personal boundaries if you're going to live a healthy life.

MY TRUE HEALING ACTION PLAN

Which of my relationships have boundary issues?

What should I do to improve boundaries in each of these relationships?

5

DEALING WITH DISAPPOINTMENTS OR BETRAYALS

―――※―――

THERE'S NO WAY TO AVOID DISAPPOINTMENTS IN LIFE, BUT there are good ways to cope with them.

When we are disappointed in a major way, we usually go through the stages of grief, which include shock, denial, anger, and sorrow. It doesn't help when someone says, "Don't worry, you'll be okay." The fact is, it hurts, and we must get through it. To move on, we cannot get stuck in disappointment. From personal experience, I know there are some things we can control and others we cannot.

A major life lesson I have learned is that when I expected something to happen and it didn't, it most likely was not supposed to happen. Instead, I gained experiences on a different path that otherwise I would have missed...

I studied and worked hard to become a doctor and a specialist. After many years, things changed in the medical profession. Managed care set in, and it seemed that how good a doctor I was did not matter as much as the financial "bottom line." I was disappointed and even disillusioned. But I came to realize there was no way I could control the wave of change that was happening. I had to handle my disappointment and fall back on what I wanted when I decided to become a doctor, which was to care for those in need and to teach them how to empower themselves in all aspects of their lives.

So I went down a different path and became a writer of articles and books on treating the whole human being as worthy of health in mind, body, and spirit. Through my writing, I'm accomplishing my original goals of healing and educating patients but in a different way.

If I had enjoyed a successful medical practice, as I originally planned, this book, the ones already written, and those to be written, would not exist. Only a few patients would have had a chance to see me on a one-on-one basis. But with my books, blogs, podcasts, and Internet presence, I am reaching people all over the world, beyond my wildest dreams, now and for years to come.

I had a patient come to me for consult who had thought she'd met the love of her life. Everything she'd been looking for in a relationship, she thought she'd found in him. Instead, she discovered he was a con artist. He betrayed her on every level—cheating, stealing, and lying. She was shocked to realize that rather than being his beloved partner, to him, she was a convenient bank account. The experience left her devastated, and she lost her trust in men in general.

We spoke about how betrayal is a major disappointment in how you think your life is or should be. It's a struggle every day to deal with the hurt, to figure out what you've learned from the experience, and then to move on without becoming cynical. It took a while, but my patient eventually realized it was a blessing to find out this man's true character before she married him. She learned more about herself, and she became more realistic and discriminating about the men she allowed into her life.

It's the little steps that count when you're getting through disappointments. Every morning, you are a different person; so don't get discouraged because every day, every little step counts. Know that one day you'll look back with a clearer understanding of the benefits that have come from the experience and the struggle. It's a matter of choosing your own *perspective*—how you think about what and why things didn't work out the way you wanted.

What helps to gain perspective? Your faith that you'll be taken care of, whatever you might have lost. Dare to dream big, but know that not all dreams are going to be fulfilled the way you expect them to be.

"For I know the plans I have for you. They are plans for good and not for disaster, to give you a future and a hope."

Jeremiah 29:11

"Weeping may last through the night, but joy comes with the morning."

Psalm 30:5

MY TRUE HEALING ACTION PLAN

What are my greatest disappointments?

What positive things or new paths did I learn from each one?

6

HOW TO DEAL WITH WORRIES

WORRY IS CONSIDERED THE BIGGEST MENTAL HEALTH DISORDER in America, according to *Worry-Free Living*—a book by Frank Minirth, Paul Meier, and Don Hawkins—and many other sources.

What exactly is worry, and why is it so dangerous?

It's a state of restlessness and agitation, producing mental disturbance, anxiety, uneasiness, apprehension, painful uncertainty, and dread. These feelings are usually the result of thoughts that something bad may happen. If uncontrolled, worry will result in anxiety disorders, panic attacks, or even mental illness.

Those who worry spend a disproportionate amount of time thinking about the future, speculating on what might occur and fearing the worst. Worry can be associated with a specific panic-inducing situation or a chronic, vague, never-ending fear that something terrible is about to happen to wreck plans. Or it can be a fear that whatever you do, you will face disapproval or will not be liked by others.

When you worry, you are all keyed up with nothing to fight or flee and no way to turn off the stress chemicals. Chronic worry puts you under chronic stress; it's like being a ticking bomb that is not allowed to explode. Every system in the body is affected by worry. In addition to raising blood pressure, you raise your risk of heart attack and stroke. Muscle tension can give rise to headaches, back pain, and other body aches. Worry can also trigger an increase in stomach acid and either slow down or speed up muscle contractions in your intestines, which can lead to stomachaches, constipation, diarrhea, gas, or heartburn, and with time, gastrointestinal reflux or GERD.

Worry can affect the skin, causing itching, breakouts, or rashes. It can also impact the respiratory system and compromise your immune system. This makes your body more vulnerable to bacteria, viruses, and perhaps even cancer.

A cause or pattern for worry may be found in the past.

Regina, a forty-seven-year-old supervisor at a small company, came to see me about excessive worry affecting her peace of mind and her sleep. About six months before, she had overheard rumors that her company was on the verge of closing down. Being a single parent with two teenagers, Regina was overwhelmed by the uncertainty of losing her job and good income.

"What will I do about health insurance? How can I keep up with the house payments? If I lose my job, how will we be able to make it? Dr. Carolle, I'm overcome with worry."

We discovered through talking that her impending job loss was rekindling the feeling of abandonment she'd experienced as a child and again later as a young mother. Now that she needed her job to survive with her children, she was going to be abandoned again. Her concern was legitimate, but obsessive worry was affecting the quality of her current life and her ability to make alternate plans. Regina was one of those patients who, because of her past history, had totally lost the faith she usually had—the knowledge she'd be taken care of, no matter what—and so she hadn't been relying on her religious beliefs in times of stress.

When Regina was five years old, her mother took her to visit her grandmother in another state. She awoke the next morning to find her mother had gone, and she was told she was going to stay with her grandmother for a while. Every day, Regina would wait at the window, hoping her mother would come back for her. When she asked about her daddy, she was told he was very sick. She was confused, desolate, and worried, even though she was well taken care of by her grandmother. Her experience of abandonment by her mother and father left deep wounds that set a pattern of worry for her life. This issue was further exacerbated when later in life her husband left her to raise two young children on her own.

Regina is not an exception. No person lives without worry, but for some, it is out of control. Many high achievers are worriers, as are many laid-back people. Each patient who comes to see me fills out a comprehensive questionnaire. There are two things almost everyone puts a checkmark next to—*weight* and *worry*.

Regina did lose her job. She survived with savings and her unemployment checks for a while. She worked with a therapist to heal the wounds from her past. She found she enjoyed spending more time with her children and started going back to church with them, even finding joy volunteering her time at church. Eventually, she came to believe that an obstacle or disaster could open the door to a better opportunity. Within six months she found a dream job with higher pay and better benefits.

When we suffer from abandonment and neglect as a child, we are in constant need of reassurance that our friends or our spouse will not leave us—unless we heal ourselves. We can choose to avoid the source of worry, by doing things such as leaving when the going gets tough, or we can face our problem, take appropriate action, heal the past, and put it behind us.

The recommendations I gave to Regina and other patients like her:

- Use therapy to console and heal your angry inner child.
- Forgive whoever abandoned you. You'll never know all the circumstances.
- Learn to surrender, and believe you will be taken care of, no matter what.
- Use relaxation techniques, such as meditation, deep breathing, and yoga.
- Focus on living in the present, not on what bad things might happen in the future.
- Develop a better connection with your higher power.

"Casting all your care upon him; for he careth for you."

Peter 5:7

*"All is well. Everything is working out for my highest good.
Out of this situation only good will come. I am safe!"*

Louise Hay

MY TRUE HEALING ACTION PLAN

What are my biggest worries?

What positive steps will I take to stop worrying?

7

HOW TO DEAL WITH REGRETS

I KNOW TOO MANY PEOPLE WHO SPEND SO MUCH TIME DWELLING on the past that the present passes them by, ruining their chance to create a better future.

One of these people, unfortunately, was my mother. I never saw her happy. Mother never forgave herself for not having the means to raise my sister and me. I was a dutiful daughter who took care of her until the end, and I tried to do everything to make her smile. But her smile never lasted for long. I told her many times that because of her sacrifices I became motivated to take charge of my life and was able to get an education. But her regret ate at her anyway.

If you are harboring regrets, here are some thoughts to consider:

- You cannot change the past. What is done is done. You cannot turn back the clock and change anything in the past, no matter how much you regret it.

- All we have is the present. This is where the action is, so "be here now."

- If you regret something, you must forgive yourself. Tell yourself you did not know any better at the time. We all make foolish mistakes, and they are part of the learning curve of life.

- Regret is a toxic emotion that affects your personality and affects the people in your life.

- Regrets hijack your emotions and interfere with your ability to focus on the positive.

- Learn from your mistakes. The worst that could happen is that you never learn from the past and repeat the same mistake again and again, creating a cycle that keeps you in an endless loop of regret.

- Have faith that what has happened was part of the lessons you were supposed to learn in this lifetime.

"Guilt serves no purpose."

"Regret is the cancer of life!"

"Today is the day to let go!"

MY TRUE HEALING ACTION PLAN

What are my biggest regrets?

Starting today, what positive steps will I take to stop regretting the past?

8

DEALING WITH PAST ISSUES OF ABUSE

———

IT HAS BEEN MY EXPERIENCE THAT THOSE CURRENTLY AND continually suffering from unresolved emotional and physical symptoms have had past experiences with abuse, especially if it occurred during childhood. The little child in them is still dealing with issues of abandonment, neglect, physical, emotional, sexual, or verbal abuse. They are also dealing with anger, resentment, and mistrust, have lost their faith in humanity, and are unable to connect to a higher power.

The younger they were and the more frequent the abuse—especially if the perpetrator was a parent or caregiver—the more these unresolved issues will resurface later in life. They appear as emotional and physical symptoms and are especially evident during stressful situations, such as if the parent, caregiver, abuser, or someone like them enters into their life. The appearance of symptoms can be likened to the body's intuitive wisdom, reminding the person that these old wounds *have to be resolved.*

During stressful moments in adult life, especially when feeling rejection, the little, hurt child will surface and again experience a deeply ingrained pain that manifests in a variety of symptoms and behaviors. Those abused by parents or primary caretakers have wounds that often manifest in things such as an inability to feel or trust, anxiety problems, depression, relationship problems, eating disorders, and alcohol or drug abuse. They live life, trying to please others, second-guessing themselves, struggling with perfectionism, a lack of confidence, emotional emptiness, image/weight issues, and difficulties with intimacy.

The hurt little child may have had parents or caretakers who were emotionally distant and/or had very high expectations. As an adult, this "inner child" will always be looking for the acknowledgment and praise they missed out on during their childhood. They are unable to say no and may stay in abusive relationships at work and at home because of lack of self-esteem.

Since everyone else is the hurt little child's mirror, they will interpret consciously or unconsciously every occurrence in life from that perspective. As adults, they always have a feeling of being abandoned and alone. Unfortunately, they will attract the types of relationships that they are accustomed to, so they are again abandoned and abused emotionally, physically, and sexually.

I know that one of the main factors keeping the hurt inner child from healing is their anger at God, especially if they were raised in a religion that teaches that they should call upon God to save them from suffering. The little child feels abandoned by everyone, including their higher power, and thus has difficulty trusting anyone.

HEALING STEPS

- Bring unresolved abuse issues to the surface. Admit that these buried,
  hurtful issues may be the cause of your emotional and physical symptoms
  in adulthood.

- Seek counseling on how to heal the traumatized inner child.

- Find a way to forgive the abuser, whether they are dead or alive.

- Consider psychotherapy.

- Develop a stronger connection with God or a higher power who will always be there for you.

MY TRUE HEALING ACTION PLAN

What issues of abuse happened in my past?

Starting today, what positive steps will I take to start healing past hurts?

9

TAKING IT ONE DAY AT A TIME

———~~———

"LIFE" HAPPENS RIGHT NOW, ONE MINUTE AT A TIME, ONE DAY AT a time. Too many of us are either thinking about the past or trying to project our future instead of living in the present moment. How often do you do this? Try to be aware of where your thoughts are, as it is a pervasive habit that makes you miss out on living in *today's precious moments*. And too quickly they become the past.

I learned from one of my spiritual mentors that when we are stuck in the past, we not only waste the present, we also waste the energy to create positive things for the future.

A while ago, one of my examination room windows overlooked a San Diego freeway. Just above the retaining wall was a large area of ice plants. Twice a year, this usually green area suddenly changed into a bed of pink blossoms. As a special treat for me, nestled among the little pink flowers were purple blossoms. For some unknown reason, admiring that purple patch always brought my thoughts back to the present and had a soothing effect upon my soul. Through the years, whenever I was overwhelmed, I would be reminded to enjoy the day when I looked at those flowers.

Deborah and Susan, mother and daughter, have been my patients for many years. One day, Deborah told me that her thirty-two-year-old daughter Susan had died. I was shocked. I know losing a child is the most painful experience a parent can endure. What could I say to Deborah? How to console her? When I told her I was sorry to hear about Susan, she smiled faintly.

"Do not worry about me," she said. "I am doing pretty well, I think. Life must go on. I have to be strong for my family, especially for my grandchildren."

"How do you do it?" I asked her. "How do you find the strength?"

"My faith sustains me, and I take it day by day," Deborah said, "One day at a time. Yes, I am sad. Sometimes, it's very hard to fall asleep. But when I'm awake, I'm thankful to God for giving me a chance to see another day, that I am alive, that my health is still good. Sometimes, you know, we are too busy in life to appreciate the little things. I have been taking my time and enjoying every little thing since Susan died.

"Look, look," she continued. "Look at those pink flowers by the freeway. I was admiring them while waiting for you. And look at that little patch of purple flowers. Isn't it beautiful? You see, Dr. Carolle, those are the little things that keep me appreciating each day."

I knew exactly what she meant.

"We lose precious time obsessing to control the future and handling the past.
Make today and every day matter for you and everyone around you.
It is not about the destination; it is about the journey."

MY TRUE HEALING ACTION PLAN

Why is it difficult for me to enjoy one day at a time?

Starting today, what positive steps will I take to focus more on each day?

10

LISTENING TO YOUR INTUITION

—⁓—

INTUITION IS A WAY OF "KNOWING BEFORE YOU KNOW" OR "THAT little voice" in your head. Learning to listen to your intuition can be a great self-protection, early-warning tool to protect your health.

Ignoring intuition about what's going on with your body can result in irritability or anxiety, and in time, heartburn, irregular bleeding, insomnia, sexual problems, or gastrointestinal problems that can be misdiagnosed as hormone imbalance, adrenal fatigue, PMS, perimenopause, or menopause.

Letting your mind listen to your internal warning systems can even save your life. Besides health warnings, your "sixth sense" can give you an idea of what to do in many circumstances. Sometimes, your intuition might cause you to delay leaving home, so you will avoid an accident, or it might keep you from signing a certain contract, etc.

Many people have not been able to let the gift of intuition blossom, especially those who have low self-esteem and don't trust themselves, or those who are told they are crazy when they share out loud.

We don't want to be overcautious or paranoid, but we should pay attention when we hear warning bells going off in our heads. How many times have you ignored your intuition? Were you ever ripped off by a "deal" even though you were forewarned by your intuition that it sounded too good to be true? What message is your mind giving you?

How do we know to trust our intuition when there is so much conflicting information out there? Who we are is a result of what has been taught to us, what we have learned over the years, and the experience of others. The inner voice we need to listen to is our higher intelligence. If we let it, it will allow us to heal the planet and ourselves, and to learn about unconditional love...

The people we are to respect and listen to have the same high-minded intuition, and their thoughts are unconditionally accepted all over the world, resonating with every culture, race, and social class. They can heal others with a smile, a touch, a look, and when you are around them, you wish you could be like them.

Being a medical intuitive—someone who can see, hear, and feel what is wrong with a patient and quickly uncover the root cause of his or her symptoms—has been a very challenging journey. How could I listen to that inner voice telling me to wait before operating on a patient who might need a Caesarean or who had a deadly condition? But my intuition has never proven me wrong. I am fortunate to have mentors help me understand my gift, which has allowed me to be the powerful intuitive healer I am today.

Have faith and trust that listening to your intuition can be a great self-protection tool. It can be the key to understanding what's affecting your body and your health, and so much more.

"Listen to your guts; if they have a queasy feeling about something, the answer is no."

"Learn to trust and listen to your inner voice; it is your best friend and has your well-being in mind."

"When at a crossroads in your life's journey, following what your gut is telling you will probably guide you in the right direction."

MY TRUE HEALING ACTION PLAN

Why don't I listen to my intuition?

Starting today, what steps will I take to start paying attention to my intuition?

11

DE-STRESSING MINDFULLY

———~~~———

STRESS IS INEVITABLE IN OUR LIVES. BUT WHEN YOU ARE OVER-stressed, it will cause emotional and physical symptoms, from anxiety to cancer. Emotional and physical symptoms are a warning signal—a way your body communicates with you.

A symptom is the tip of the iceberg, pointing to something deeper; true healing can only occur when the root cause is found and dealt with. Listen to your body when it lets you know you're over-stressed. It is your inner wisdom talking to you.

When you feel stressed, make time to take a "life inventory." Figure out what your strongest stress triggers are. They usually involve your outlook on life, an imbalance in your personal relationships, work/career, finances, or your lack of spiritual health.

Are you in the right relationship? Is your present job a good fit for you? Stress can be related to your environment or to the side effects of a medication. Good mental health depends on healthy relationships that nurture you. This means establishing healthy boundaries in all of them.

Know your limitations when it comes to your work and career. Is it the major stressor in your life? Are you doing what you love? Does it fulfill your needs and that of those you love? Do you have all the tools you need? Do you need to ask for help?

It is very important to acknowledge how you respond when under stress. See if you deal with it in a negative manner by doing things such as overeating, over-exercising, or using mood-altering substances, etc.

Please have faith, and trust that you will be taken care of, no matter what, in spite of how things may look. Don't be like the many patients I see who stay in unfulfilling jobs or relationships until they become very sick and reach a point of no return. Please practice believing deep within yourself that you deserve better...and that when a door closes, another one always opens for your highest good.

Steps for de-stressing mindfully include, biofeedback, yoga, getting a massage, exercising, herbal teas, a relaxing bath, time alone or with a friend or a pet or a loved one. Others, such as meditation, listening to music, reading, and the power of prayer are discussed within this book.

"Leave the past behind, so you can be free to enjoy the present."

"Live in the moment; don't waste time dwelling in the past.
I choose how I live my life moment by moment."

MY TRUE HEALING ACTION PLAN

What are my stress triggers?

Starting today, what steps will I take to avoid/handle/release my stress triggers?

12

Learning to "Be in the Moment"

——⁓——

MOST OF US ARE FOCUSED ON THINGS FROM THE PAST, OR WE ARE thinking/worrying about the future. This gives us a distracted, poor quality of present life, increases stress, and, eventually, it leads to physical and emotional symptoms.

Being mindfully in the moment means being aware of your thoughts and what's going on around you. Learning to be in the moment or living in the present is a gift you can give yourself.

Praying, meditating, focusing on one's breathing or an object in front of you will usually work to bring your attention back into the present. Chew slowly while eating, and be mindful of each bite, listen to the sounds as you walk, focus on one task at a time. Treat your wandering mind like an unruly child, and gently remind it to *pay attention*!

I've learned that sometimes it may take something drastic to be able to be in the moment...

When I had my bout with panic attacks, I was full of fear without any reason. I heard that the fear of having a panic attack could itself cause you to have one. The night that it first happened, I was at my brother Lesly's house in New York in the middle of the night in July 2000. I called my therapist Denise who told me to get him on the phone. I didn't want to; he had to get up at 5:00 a.m. But reluctantly, I went to his room, woke him, and handed him the phone. I vaguely remember him putting ice into my hands, watching it melt as soon as it hit my skin, the water dripping through my fingers and onto the pile of towels his wife Louana kept replacing. I could see how they were looking at me in disbelief. I was no longer the take-charge big sister; I was a frightened little girl who just wanted to curl up and ask for help. But the burning sensation of the ice on my hands helped to keep me focused on the present until the panic subsided.

I continued to work with Denise, and from her I learned about the "fight-or-flight response." Whenever there is a perceived harmful event, attack, or threat to survival, the body prepares immediately for rigorous physical activity, to fight or to flee. A physiological reaction ensues; the adrenals release epinephrine, also known as adrenaline, resulting in a fast increase in heart rate and blood pressure, elevation of glucose levels in the blood, and redistribution of blood from the digestive tract to the muscles.

These frightening physiological changes, occurring during the fight or flight response, are activated in order to give the body increased strength and speed, but they often are not appropriate to the situation.

Focus on your breathing or something else that helps to keep you be in the moment, and ride out your body's reaction, and you will able to control your reaction in stressful moments and prevent panic attacks.

A month later, I went to a movie with my husband Albert. All of a sudden, I heard a voice whispering in my head. *It's so dark in here! Don't you need to go out for some fresh air?*

My heart started to race, and I was overcome by intense fear. I couldn't believe it; I had been able to fly all the way to Haiti and back without a panic attack. *Why now?* I wondered. *Why here?*

The dread wouldn't go away. The only way I could possibly relieve it was to get out of the movie theater. Fast. But I knew if I did, I would never again be able to go to a movie, fly on an airplane, or be in any enclosed place. So I decided to stay and get through the attack.

While focusing on my breathing, I grabbed Albert's hand and squeezed it.

The more discomfort I experienced, the harder I squeezed. I thrashed around so much I was almost kneeling in the small space in front of me, but I didn't give up. I called on the power of all my spiritual connections and prayed.

The attack passed. I took deep breaths, slid back into my seat, and continued to watch the movie.

I have not had another panic attack since.

The following is a series of steps that will help you "be in the moment."

THE POWER OF THE BREATHING

Breathing oxygen and exhaling carbon dioxide is what keeps us alive. When we're under stress, our breathing becomes shallow. In a tense situation, we might even hold our breath for longer than we realize.

Consciously, purposefully taking slow, deep breaths will relax both your body and your mind and will return you to the present moment.

Whenever you are stressed, do this: While comfortably seated, close your eyes, and begin taking slow, deep breaths through your mouth, slowly exhaling through your nose. Meanwhile, visualize each part of your body going limp, starting with the top of the head, proceeding down to your toes. *Do not forget to stay aware of and in control of your breathing.*

I practice this technique very often by myself and together with patients who are going through a stressful period in their lives. I promise you that breathing slowly and deeply can help in any situation where you want to calm down and stay focused in the present. Have faith that taking time to breathe, time without the burden of expectation, will make you feel much better.

"Amidst the chaos around you or in your mind, just close your eyes and focus on each breath, in...and out...and reclaim your peace!"

MY TRUE HEALING ACTION PLAN

Am I aware of the way I breathe and how important it is to my health?

Starting today, what will I do to become aware of and slow down my breathing?

THE POWER OF DANCING

"Whenever you feel sad," my father used to tell me, "just put on some music, and start dancing."

Around the world, dancing has been an important component of many religious rituals. It is not only a way to stay in shape but a way to align the body and the soul and to be connected with the sacred as well as with others. As you let go and concentrate on the rhythm of the beats, you can only be in the moment.

I come from a culture where people "dance their troubles away." We have carnivals in Haiti, and weeks in advance of the festivities that end on Mardi Gras bands roam the streets, playing their new songs. People follow, singing and always dancing. "Good girls" like me weren't supposed to join in, but I would find a way to escape and do so!

While nurturing a broken heart in medical school, I took dance lessons, joining the *Grupo Baile Folclorico*. I practiced at home until my roommate Nicole said either stop or she was going to strangle me.

"We're here to become doctors, not dancers," she said. "I need peace and quiet to study."

She was probably right; the *zapateando* was as noisy as tap-dancing but oh-so-healing for my heart and soul.

During my last year of residency training at Mount Sinai in Milwaukee, to keep my sanity, I started to take belly-dancing classes and even performed at the farewell party for the chief residents. At all the nurses' stations were party invitations that said: There will be a performance by our famous belly-dancer doctor!

When I found myself heartbroken again in San Diego, while trying to start a private practice as an OB-GYN, I resumed belly-dancing lessons and participated in a first-ever video in 1985. Subsequently, in 1991, I was called by the TV show Entertainment Tonight. They'd seen the video *Atea and Friends* and were doing a show about the beneficial effects of belly dancing. They wanted to interview me, a belly-dancing doctor. Who could have guessed that the video made so many years ago would land me a spot on national television? I was so excited to share the healing benefits of dancing.

Wherever you are, regardless of your physical limitations, you can dance!

A dear friend's father who was a great dancer became wheelchair-bound. He loved to dance, started when he was young and continued to do so until he no longer could. I could see the sadness in his face while there were people dancing around. I walked over to him and asked him for a dance. He had a perplexed look on his face until I showed him how to use his electric wheelchair's button to maneuver while I twirled around him. He was elated and became the greatest wheelchair dancer. No one could stop him until he finally passed away. For years, his family would recall the new lease on life he got by learning how to dance in his wheelchair.

Whenever I feel overwhelmed, I put on one of my favorite songs, sing, cry, and dance my heart out, and I encourage you to do the same.

"To the Universe belongs the dancer.
He who does not dance does not know what happens."

Gnostic gospel Acts of John.

"Dance when you're broken up.
Dance if you've torn the bandage off.
Dance in the middle of the fighting.
Dance in your blood.
Dance when you're perfectly free."

Rumi

MY TRUE HEALING ACTION PLAN

What music or songs make me tap my feet and want to dance?

Starting today, what will I do to benefit from the power of dancing?

THE POWER OF GARDENING

Gardening offers the benefits of regular exercise in fresh air, with natural vitamin D from the sun. It is an enjoyable way to exercise for all ages without adding undo stress to your body. It involves a lot of stretching and repetitive movements and even resistance principles similar to weight training.

Gardening helps build strong bones to prevent osteoporosis, provides a chance to work off extra calories, and helps you stay limber. Exercising in nature is a good way to improve your mood. It increases the release of endorphins, the feel-good hormones.

Not only does having your own garden offer the satisfaction of watching something take root and grow, it is an opportunity to introduce children to the joys of nature. Besides getting you closer to nature, tending to plants also beautifies your home and improves property values.

At a particularly stressful time in my life, something compelled me to take up gardening to clear my head. I was deciding whether to quit private practice as a holistic gynecologist and be an intuitive consultant for midlife women. I started digging and planting, and now, years later, I have a beautiful botanical garden. My garden has not only provided me with flowers, fresh fruits, herbs, and vegetables, it also offers others and me a place to replenish the soul.

Whenever I take a stroll in my garden, I experience a sense of peace and also excitement about the life I watch growing around me. Each time is full of surprises—the burgeoning of the deciduous trees during spring, bright yellow, honey, and blue irises, fragrant roses that keep on blooming. It seems the lizards know when I am coming and cannot help darting along my path. The many birds sound like a beautiful orchestra. How can I worry when I watch them totally free? I talk to my plants and trees, thanking them for offering me so much beauty. No wonder they thrive... As with all living things, I think they can feel the love, and they return it.

I find my garden so beneficial to my peace of mind and spirit—while in it I feel totally connected to God. On many occasions, I have shared it with those who come and spend time with me in my healing center. What a great way to be with your doctor, instead of inside a sterile office. The first hour or more of our encounter is spent walking around, pulling a few weeds, gathering fresh fruits and flowers. During the rest of their stay, we spend most of our time together in the garden. When I do healing retreats, guests can choose a special spot to be alone, breathe the fresh air, and reflect on what we've discussed as they make sense of their lives.

Being in the garden gives me a beautiful balance with work. It is mentally beneficial both for me and my patients. It calms the mind, and when the mind calms, the soul is more at peace. Before my guests leave, we take cuttings from the numerous succulents, cacti, and flowers, and I put them in a beautiful pot so they can take home a little bit of the peace of mind they've found here.

If you choose to start or improve a garden, you need to be careful, and listen to your body. As with any kind of exercise, it should be done in moderation. Many gardening tasks require kneeling, sitting, standing, and squatting that can put unnecessary stress and strain on the knees and back. I built raised garden beds to reduce bending.

There are so many benefits to gardening. Creating and tending a garden not only provides you with fresh, healthy things to eat; there are also specific mental, physical, and spiritual benefits.

There are few things more peaceful, satisfying, and even healing than being in nature, watching your plants and flowers grow. While gardening, you are connected with nature; you live in the moment and are restored by it.

You can start a garden anywhere—indoors or out—with very little space. I happen to be living in beautiful San Diego, but an indoor garden can be enjoyed all year long! Check on the Internet or at a local plant nursery for advice and supplies.

For the health of your mind, bodies and spirit, plant something wonderful in the garden of your life.

"The earth is full of the goodness of the Lord."

Psalm33.5

MY TRUE HEALING ACTION PLAN

Can I see the benefit of gardening for me?

Starting today, what will I do to proceed?

BENEFITS OF A HOBBY

Having a hobby—and I mean a healthy one—is enriching and will help keep your life balanced. Several research studies have shown that people who engage in hobbies are less likely to develop memory problems. Hobbies are also known to stave off depression and lower blood pressure.

Investing time in an enjoyable hobby by yourself or in a group or club is like a mini vacation from your daily worries and challenges; plus it's a great way to socialize and meet people who share your interest. A hobby can bring out a creative you (sketching, photography, crafts), be relaxing and a way to meditate (yoga, fishing, gardening), something that keeps you fit (tennis, swimming, biking, traveling), or develops a talent (singing, playing an instrument). Above all, it should be something that makes you *happy*.

One day, a patient came to see me, saying she feared "something was wrong" with her, but she could not pinpoint what it was. She had been my patient for many years; I delivered her children, now ages sixteen and fourteen. I knew she had been a good stay-at-home mom, taking the kids everywhere and supporting them in everything they wished to do. I remembered that she used to love to sing in a choir, but she said she had no time anymore for choir practice.

I examined her and sent her home with a written prescription: *Choir practice weekly.* I told her she had to find the time to go to choir practice. She was ordered to call me in a month. She called three weeks later. She had gone back to choir practice and was feeling much better.

I have many hobbies, and they've change throughout the years, from belly dancing, to painting on canvas, designing and planting a one-acre botanical garden, etc.

In 2011, I was the apprentice of Salvador Roberto Torres, a world-famous Chicano muralist in San Diego with whom I spent eight months restoring the historical Kelco mural in an area of San Diego called Barrio Logan. I had my own fish—a clown wrasse measuring nine feet long and five feet high. I also helped with other fish and a coral bed that was added where several huge doors had been turned into a wall.

With Maestro Torres, I learned to follow orders. Instead of being the surgeon, the leader of the band, the expert, I watched and learned how to mix colors, properly clean paint brushes and store them, while making beautiful art pieces.

Later on, I worked with Mr. Torres, Ayanna Bassiouni, and Kraig Blue, all fine-art artists. With their participation and guidance, I turned my healing center into a museum, where most of the walls around the pool have either mixed-media murals or goddesses. It is a work in progress, and sometimes, patients participate in adding to the murals as a form of art therapy. Being involved in such beautiful creation reminds them of the presence of God.

So take a class, learn to play an instrument, just do whatever it is that you've "*put on the back burner until later when blah, blah, blah...*"

MY TRUE HEALING ACTION PLAN

What hobbies am I interested in?

Starting today, what steps will I take to make time for at least one pleasurable hobby?

THE POWER OF MEDITATING

People have practiced meditation for thousands of years in order to promote spiritual, emotional, and physical well-being. Meditation is a state of quiet contemplation, a great way to keep you in the present. Much research on its benefits look at what is known as *mindful meditation*, where you focus on your breathing to stay in the moment. When thoughts intrude, let them go—one way is to put them inside a balloon and release them to float away—and then refocus on breathing gently and deeply.

Other types of meditation include *compassionate meditation*, where people focus on kind, loving thoughts, or *mantra meditation*, where you repeat a sacred or spiritual saying to feel closer to God.

Did you know that being in a meditative state reduces your body's blood levels of stress hormones such as cortisol and adrenaline? In AsapScience's *The Scientific Power of Meditation,* Mitchell Moffit and Gregory Brown thoroughly explain how meditation yields a number of benefits, including the ability to fight—not cure—diseases, increase empathy, and even lead to physical changes in the brain.

Studies show that meditation causes a reduction in heart rate, respiration rate, and pulse rate, creating a feeling of relaxation. Meditation increases alpha brain waves, which are known to reduce feelings of negative mood, tension, sadness, and anger.

Meditating twenty minutes, once or twice a day, can decrease blood pressure significantly. Daily meditation is very useful to relieve stress and panic disorders. Meditators are better able to handle difficult situations, report a higher general happiness measure, and a higher level of spiritual consciousness.

I highly recommend making meditation a part of your life.

MY TRUE HEALING ACTION PLAN

What do I know about the benefits of meditation?

Starting today, what steps will I take to add meditation to my life?

THE POWER OF MUSIC

In addition to music being enjoyable, relaxing, or energizing, I believe it has the power to facilitate spiritual awakening and healing. It is a powerful tool that can transform the human condition. Throughout history, music has been used in a variety of ways, from ceremony and ritual to celebration and enjoyment.

Music inspires and uplifts, drawing us closer to the divine; it heals our emotional selves and creates a bond with others.

My father loved music and had recordings in many languages. He told me, "If you feel sad, play some good music." I've followed Father's advice so many times over the years and find myself singing while tears roll down my cheeks. When the song is over, I'm totally relieved of whatever was bothering me.

One summer evening, I was listening to the San Diego Symphony Orchestra at the Embarcadero open-air theater. The sky was full of stars. On each table sat a small vase with a candle. The Romeros, a family of four generations of classical guitar players, also entertained that night. When they played one of my favorites, *Aranjuez*, the music went straight to my heart.

If there is a heaven on Earth, this is it, I thought to myself. When the concert ended, I felt like screaming. Then something unexpected occurred. One person in the audience started to scream, then more and more, and soon all of us were screaming. The music awakened something so powerful in that audience that "Bravo" would not have sufficed.

Not only can music move your soul and be inspirational, but also there are scientific experiments that prove the vibrations of different music affects the growth of plants.

Why not humans, too, and why not *you*?

> *"God sent His singers upon earth with songs of gladness and of mirth that they might touch the hearts of men, and bring them back to heaven again."*
>
> Henry Wadsworth Longfellow

MY TRUE HEALING ACTION PLAN

What is my favorite music?

Starting today, what steps will I take to use music as a healing method?

THE HEALING POWERS OF NATURE

When we experience worry, uncertainty, grief, or sorrow, our focus tends to narrow. Taking some time to look around and enjoy nature can help us to heal. Hippocrates, the father of modern medicine, recognized this powerful attribute in his humbling statement: *"Nature cures; not the physician."*

When in nature, you become aware of the infinite circle of life. There is evidence of decay, destruction, and death, but there are also examples of rejuvenation, restoration, and renewal. The never-ending cycle of birth, life, death, and rebirth in nature can help you put life and death into perspective.

I learned long ago that spending time in my garden is one of the best things I can do for myself, especially when overwhelmed or stressed. It gives me a beautiful balance with work and a personal window into the world of nature...

One day, while working in my garden, I witnessed something wonderful. A dozen small birds were playing a game. Each bird stood on the ground about a foot away from the next one. Close to my fence is a twelve-foot-tall hedge, and one by one, each bird flew straight into this hedge, hitting it head-on. Some birds reached the top, some only the middle. They buried themselves within the foliage, screaming and screeching. When they grew tired, they flew back to the ground. Then the routine began again. The creatures of nature can even remind our spirits to play.

Since 1999, I have made many trips to my native country of Haiti, along with a team of volunteers who provide free medical care and coordinate projects for the children. La Vallée de Jacmel is a small town nestled in a chain of mountains, overlooking the Caribbean Sea in the southeastern part of Haiti. There is something magical about the sky, the clouds, the gentle winds, and the calm sea far away.

During my visits, I spend long hours at the hospital and with the children. In the evenings, I meet with village leaders to prioritize the few resources we bring to share. One night, I went to bed around midnight, wondering if I would have the strength to accomplish all I had scheduled the next day. I awoke after only a few hours of sleep and went to my balcony, overlooking a cliff. While everyone else slept, I sat and communed with nature. No lights disturbed the night, as the generator only operates between six and nine o'clock in the evening. As my eyes adjusted, I saw stars all around me, millions of them.

Overwhelmed by my tiredness and the beauty that surrounded me, I began to cry. My tears were for my vision of improving the living conditions that surrounded me and for thoughts of the demanding days ahead. But my tears soon dried, and my soul was fed by the joy of witnessing this beauty of nature.

> *"Nature is the one place where miracles not only happen, but they happen all the time."*
>
> Thomas Wolfe

> *"Look deep, deep into nature, and then you will understand everything better."*
>
> Albert Einstein

MY TRUE HEALING ACTION PLAN

For me, what's the best part about being in nature?

Starting today, what steps will I take to use nature as a healing respite?

THE POWER OF SINGING

I personally love the following quote from Saint Therese of Liseaux, especially because singing has been and still is a joyous part of my life.

"Allow your soul the freedom to sing, dance, praise, and love. It is there for each and every one of us."

I sang in a church choir for years as a teenager in Haiti and am sure it kept me out of trouble. I also learned folkloric songs and their respective dances and would participate in art and theater performances. Listening to the radio and singing along to various songs helped me become proficient in Spanish, English, and Italian.

Now a member of the One Heart One Mind Church choir in San Diego—yes, I am a soprano, and my voice is getting better and better as the days go by—I appreciate that learning new religious songs based on scriptures strengthens my faith.

Whenever I feel overwhelmed, there are many songs that make me feel closer to God but none like *Ave Maria* or *Total Praise* or when Charles Aznavour—the French equivalent of Frank Sinatra—sings *Merci Mon Dieu,* and I sing along with him.

My heart was lost until you showed me the way.
A path full of hope that fills empty dreams with desire to live.
Thank-you God.
What I was hoping to achieve on this earth
And that I prayed for
You made it happen.
Since I found love and happiness
I want to say with all my heart
Thank-you God.

MY TRUE HEALING ACTION PLAN

What songs touch me deeply?

Starting today, what steps will I take to sing more?

The Power of Writing

Keeping a journal helps you to open your mind and find out what's *really* going on within you.

After my bout with panic attacks in 2000, my therapist gave me a journal to write in as part of my homework. I wrote down everything that was bothering me.

Putting these issues into words and seeing them on paper helps you to view your problems more clearly. The many benefits of keeping a journal include:

- Writing things down puts them into perspective.
- Compiling a list of possible options for each problem or challenge creates an action plan.
- It helps clarify your thinking and promotes self-knowledge.
- It decreases the intensity of emotions, which decreases your stress and helps you stay in the present.
- It can make you happier if you also write about what you are grateful for.

But don't limit your writing to personal journaling. You can write about anything and in any style, including poetry, songs, articles, editorials to the newspaper, a blog, or whatever you enjoy.

Writing has helped me stay grounded over the years. I started writing my first book in Spanish in 1994 when I was asked to write a column for the *Baja California Diario*. Since then, I have written many award-winning how-to books in English, French, and Haitian Kréyol—which I either self-published or placed with a major publisher such as Hay House.

One day, a friend, Dr. Marlene Racine-Toussaint of the *Multicultural Women Presence*, told me she was putting together a book of poems written in French, English, and Kréyol called *Brassage - Une Anthologie Poétique De Femmes Haitiennes—An Anthology of Poems of Haitian Women*—and she asked me to contribute at least four poems.

"I'm not a poet," I told her.

"You have to trust that you are and just start writing," she said with confidence.

As I sat in front of my computer, eventually, the words just flowed, and in no time the poems were written. Doing it gave me the opportunity to heal some painful emotions through my words. One was so poignant that it was chosen to be read at the book signing.

Writing can give you better perspective about your life. In particular, I believe that writing about stressful events helps you come to terms with them, reducing the impact of these stressors on your physical and mental health.

MY TRUE HEALING ACTION PLAN

What kind of writing could I incorporate into my life?

What kind might I enjoy?

Starting today, what steps will I take to start incorporating writing into my life?

13

PRACTICING FORGIVENESS

FORGIVENESS IS A DECISION TO LET GO OF HURT AND RESENTMENT and thoughts of revenge. Those who live to seek revenge live in the past, degrading the present. Individuals who harbor anger and hate increase their risk of heart attack and decrease the response capacity of their immune systems.

Once you forgive, anger is decreased, you feel better about yourself, and personal relationships are enhanced. Studies have documented the psychological benefits of forgiveness, such as reduced anxiety, less stress, and less depression.

Forgiveness is recognizing you have been wronged, giving up all resulting resentment, and eventually responding to the offending person with compassion. It does not mean you deny you have been wronged, nor is it condoning or excusing your abuse. You can forgive the person without excusing the act. True forgiveness is letting go of the anger and negative feelings associated with the person or situation from the past and moving on.

The importance of forgiveness is not new and has been upheld by many of the world's religions. In Christianity, Jesus embodies forgiveness, and he practiced and preached it all the way to the cross. In Judaism, Yom Kippur is a day to atone for the sins of the past year by first seeking reconciliation with any person one has wronged, and righting the wrong if possible.

Many of my patients who were abused physically, mentally, or sexually, carry a psychological burden throughout their lives that stops them from having healthy relationships with their children, peers, and intimate partners. Carrying that burden causes them to have anxiety, anger, depression, and other mental and physical symptoms. Past abuse is often their reason to renounce religion, spirituality, and God.

I lived with my paternal grandmother and her daughter Tatante from age four until I left Haiti for the U.S. at the age of twenty. Tatante was verbally and physically abusive. After Grandma's death, she came to live with me for a while; she was seventy-one years old and had nowhere else to go. Unfortunately, she had not changed, and I felt enmity toward her that I couldn't control. I fantasized more than once that I would go to her room one day soon and find her dead.

I knew I couldn't live with these feelings, so I decided to try something I had read about. The idea is to *indirectly* confront the person you wish to forgive by writing down everything about how that person has wronged you. I used this process to successfully forgive Tatante.

HERE'S HOW THE "FORGIVING EXERCISE" WORKS:

Write down everything you feel the person has done wrong to you. Get it all out—be as specific as possible.

I wrote a long list about Tatante.

Now practice telling the person everything you want him or her to know. If you were a child when you were hurt, then the confident, grown-up you—who is not afraid of that person—takes the shy, scared child onto your lap and has the child tell it all.

When it was time to read my list indirectly to Tatante, I realized that the hurt started when I was four years old. I pictured Ti-Ca—my nickname as a little girl—on my lap and had her read the list to Tatante.

Try to think of any positive things that the person who hurt you has done for you. If there are none, that's okay. But if you keep thinking, you may remember some kindness.

I was surprised to realize that Tatante had done many positive things for me. For many years, my sister and I stayed at her house. She would feed us, pay our tuition, pay for uniforms, books, tutors, and other things for school when my father could not afford to do so.

Lastly, practice telling the person you forgive him or her because they did not know any better.

By the time I got to this part. I was sobbing. I cried for a while, letting the tears clean my soul. When I was done crying, I felt a huge weight lift from my heart and my body.

The next time I went to Florida to visit my sister Marise and Tatante, who was now living with her, we had a great time together. I saw Tatante one more time, months later during a stopover on my way to Haiti. She prepared my favorite meal and helped me rearrange my luggage. I told her I loved her, and I really meant it. Three weeks later, she became gravely ill and passed away. I went back for her funeral. At the wake, I looked at her lying in her coffin and felt there was no more hurt, no more hate, just love and gratitude. Tatante never understood why I resented her. She felt she had done her best. Forgiving her not only gave me a chance to heal, it gave her the opportunity to enjoy the company of a niece she loved in her own way.

I recommend making a list of everyone you feel has wronged you, and do the forgiveness exercise for each one. When you're ready, actively choose to forgive the person who offended you. Move away from your role as victim, and release the control and power the offending person and situation have had in your life. As you let go, you'll no longer define your life by how you've been hurt.

Forgiveness will improve the quality of your relationships and free your spirit to have a clearer connection to a higher power.

Please be aware that this forgiveness exercise can bring up painful memories, and you may need the help of a therapist to get through it.

"Forgiveness is freeing—for yourself as well as for others. It frees you from carrying the burden of past resentments. It allows you to release the past, so all your energy can be fully available for the present. Forgiveness is the ultimate gift you can give yourself."

"To be forever free, voice words of forgiveness toward anyone you have beenholding hostage in the prison of your heart."

"Anger, hostility, and rage are the worst emotions; they generate extreme stress reactions that are detrimental to your mind and body."

"Forgive the aggressor! Otherwise, you are being victimized over and over and over!"

MY TRUE HEALING ACTION PLAN

Who do I need to forgive?

Starting today, what steps will I take on the path to forgiveness?

14

Using Positive Affirmations

———

USING AFFIRMATIONS IS THE PRACTICE OF SELF-EMPOWERMENT through positive thinking—the belief that a positive mental attitude supported by affirmations creates a better, happier, healthier life.

Our belief creates every aspect of our reality. In his book, *The Biology of Belief,* Dr. Bruce Lipton writes about his research, showing that genes and DNA do not control our biology; instead, DNA is controlled by signals from outside the cell, including the energetic messages coming from our positive and negative thoughts. He suggests our body can be changed as we retrain our thinking.

My friend Louise Hay wrote her best-selling book, *You Can Heal Your Life,* in 1984 and over fifty million copies have been sold since then. The key premise of this book is that physical illnesses have their root causes in emotional and spiritual aspects of the mind and its beliefs and thought processes, and the most fundamental way to affect positive change in the body is to change the way we think, using tools such as affirmations.

Affirmations are basically a form of auto-suggestions, and when practiced deliberately and repeatedly, they reinforce chemical pathways in the brain, strengthening neural connections.

Says David J. Hellerstein, M.D., Professor of Clinical Psychiatry at Columbia University, "In brief, we have realized that 'neuroplasticity,' the ongoing remodeling of brain structure and function, occurs throughout life. It can be affected by life experiences, genes, biological agents, and by behavior, as well as by *thought patterns.*"

Those who pray with faith are using positive affirmations. Grandma's favorite affirmation when the going got tough was, *"This too shall pass...this too shall pass..."* My favorite one from Louise Hay that I have my patients use in times of chaos is, *"All is well... All is well..."* while focusing on your breathing.

Here are a few positive affirmations you can practice to rewire your brain and change your life.

"By allowing myself to be happy, I inspire others to be happy, too; I find pleasure in the simple things in life; I have healthy boundaries with my partner, friends, family, and work; I am fully present in all of my relationships; I know what I need to do to achieve success; I fully accept myself and know I'm worthy of happiness; I know how to nourish my body with healthy food; I sleep well and awaken feeling rested and energetic; I respond peacefully in all situations"

Please create a list of affirmations for yourself, and choose one or two to focus on for a few weeks at a time. Say the affirmation out loud in a confident voice several times a day and before you go to bed. To add more power to the affirmation, write it down as you speak it. Make your affirmation in the present tense, as though it is a current reality.

MY TRUE HEALING ACTION PLAN

Am I aware of what my thinking is affirming?

What positive affirmations can I create for myself to help me with my negative thoughts?

Starting today, what steps will I take to use more positive affirmations?

15

THE BENEFITS OF SHEDDING TEARS

DID YOU KNOW CRYING RELEASES TOXINS FROM YOUR BODY? When toxins build up over a period of time, they can cause illness. Many illnesses are now being recognized as the result of emotions that have been ignored for years.

Shedding emotional tears has special health benefits. Biochemist and "tear expert" Dr. William Frey at the Ramsey Medical Center in Minneapolis discovered that reflex tears are ninety-eight percent water, whereas emotional tears also contain stress hormones that get excreted from the body through crying.

Glen Dawdson, MD, studied the effects of tears because he believed they were important to the healing process. In his study, participants who wept openly and freely after the death of a spouse recovered from the grief and depression at a much faster rate than those who did not.

Confronting your emotions and allowing yourself to shed tears requires strength in the form of vulnerability. Acknowledging your deepest feelings helps you move forward in life.

My vulnerability sometimes comes in the middle of the night when I wake with a sense of doom. I feel so overwhelmed that I cannot stay in the dark and have to turn on the light. I lie still, take deep breaths, and concentrate on my breathing.

I start to pray, sometimes getting on my knees next to the bed. I'm guided to instant relief—a good cry. So I surrender and let the tears flow abundantly. The more I cry, the better I feel, and then I go back to sleeping peacefully.

Dealing with stress and expressing vulnerable emotions is hard for women and can be even harder for men. It's okay for a woman to cry, to admit something is wrong, to find solace with a friend, or seek professional help. Society makes it difficult for men to allow themselves to do these things. "Men don't cry," they say.

But it doesn't matter if you're a man or a woman; you are a human with feelings. When you feel overwhelmed, when you are emotionally and physically suffering, just surrender, let the tears flow, and have faith that this is a healthy release for your mind, body, and spirit.

"A time to weep and a time to laugh, a time to mourn and a time to dance."

Ecclesiastes 3:4

MY TRUE HEALING ACTION PLAN

When do I shed tears?

Starting today, what steps will I take to allow myself to cry for relief?

16

DON'T BE AFRAID TO ASK FOR HELP

———◦◦◦———

THERE CAN BE MANY REASONS YOU HESITATE TO ASK FOR HELP when you feel overwhelmed, stressed, or depressed. You may be embarrassed, feel guilty, or worrying it's a sign of weakness, incompetence, or selfishness.

So what can you do to get past your fear of asking for help? Please consider these reasonable statements:

- Realize it is a fear, and fear, as with any emotion, can be overcome
- Fear of being a burden is usually unfounded, as people like to feel needed
- Fear of rejection doesn't usually apply, especially when you seek help from a trained professional
- Fear of seeming weak or incapable is not appropriate when you really need help
- Fear of losing control—asking for help is a step that means quite the opposite; *asking for help is taking control.*

Your mind must allow "tune ups" when you're overwhelmed or if you feel depressed. In my opinion, asking for help in these situations is no different from taking my car to the mechanic or calling my tech guy when something goes wrong with my computer. It wasn't easy, but I've learned how to ask for help when necessary from family, friends, colleagues, and even a professional therapist.

I was close to turning fifty when I found a good therapist who did not believe that suffering unusual but frightening panic attacks had anything to do with my hormones, perimenopause, or menopause. She helped me get to the root cause of deeply buried emotional issues. I had to learn how to confront my demons, learn to forgive, plus develop coping skills that helped immediately and that will serve me for the rest of my life.

I learned and practiced what she taught me, sometimes taking one step forward and two steps backward. But I persevered because not only did I not want to suffer, I wanted to be a role model for my family, patients, and friends. Now I have a great life and can say that one of the secrets to keeping it in balance is asking for help.

You should never be afraid to ask for help from doctors, experts, friends, and God. Have faith that you were not meant to face your battles alone.

"Seeking help is a sign of strength and a willingness to grow."

Louise Hay

"Ask, and it shall be given you; seek, and ye shall find; knock, and it shall be opened unto you."

Matthew 7:7

MY TRUE HEALING ACTION PLAN

Why do I hesitate to ask for help?

Starting today, what steps will I take to allow myself to ask for help?

17

THE POWER OF TRUE FRIENDSHIP

———

A TRUE FRIEND IS SOMEONE WHO ACCEPTS YOU FOR WHO YOU are, is honest with you, is someone you can trust, and is there when you are in need. A true friend shows they value your friendship.

According to Jan Yager, author of *"Friendshifts: The Power of Friendship and How It Shapes Our Lives,* the right friends can help you feel worthwhile. She says, "School, work, parenting, and even old age are better and more fun when shared with friends."

Friendships, especially between women, can be our mirror and help us shape who we are and who we will become. Friendship can be the balm in our lives when the going gets tough, a shoulder to cry on when our intimate relationships go sour, and someone to share our joy when things go right.

In a British study, a group of chronically depressed women living in London were either assigned to a volunteer "befriender" or placed on a waiting list for one. The befrienders were instructed to be confidantes to them and meet regularly for a year. About seventy-five percent of those who had a befriender experienced a remission in depression compared to forty-five percent of those who did not. That's about the same success rate as antidepressants or cognitive therapy, but much healthier.

According to a recent poll reported in the American Sociological Review, Americans, regardless of gender, race, age, or education level, said they had only two close friends, compared to a poll in 1985 saying they had three close friends. About one in four had no one with whom they could discuss important matters.

This unfortunate decline in close, personal friends has been attributed to a number of reasons: people work longer hours and commute longer distances; women who work outside the home are also busy tending to family chores; those who do not work tend to the children and spend much time chauffeuring them to activities and lessons, and people are spending more and more time on the computer and other electronic devices, rather than spending time in person with friends.

I've noticed this worrisome trend among the men and women who seek my help to try to make sense of their lives. Most of them have all the materialist trappings but do not have any close friends; often, they also do not have close ties with their families. They do, however, say they spend time engaging with many "friends" in social media.

I am not alone in my opinion that in order to stay healthy we must make, cultivate, and keep good friends in our lives. Here are some tips to keep your friendships healthy, so they can keep you healthy, too:

- Before you can be a good friend, you have to be your own best friend. This means taking the time to nurture yourself, forgive yourself, and heal any childhood traumas that are causing you to be unhealthy.

- You need to be able to love and accept yourself as you are; otherwise, you will not be able to love and accept others as they are.

- As you grow older, your parents, siblings, relatives, and old friends can become your best friends. Take time to forgive them for past hurts and make amends.

- Each friend can support you in a different aspect of your life.

- As a woman, it can be difficult to understand a man's thoughts and behaviors and vice versa. Having friends of both sexes to help you sort things out is invaluable.

- Friendships must be nurtured.

- Friendships must be reciprocated.

- Being a good friend means knowing when to talk and when to listen.

- Be honest with your friends, speak up when something is bothering you, and expect your friends to do the same.

- Take the time frequently to let your friends know how important they are to you.

- Friends come into your life for a reason, a season, or for a lifetime. It's okay to let a friend go if you grow apart.

- Be receptive to new friends throughout your life, as your lifestyle and interests change.

- I am especially lucky to have a network of friends of all cultural backgrounds, social classes, and races in the four countries where I've lived. I also have a very close relationship with my siblings and other family members.

- In general, those who have a network of friends with whom they socialize regularly—not only on the Internet—are less likely to be sick or depressed compared with those who keep to themselves.

- That's another reason to count your friends as blessings.

- If you are not fortunate to have at least three people in your life you can call true friends, it is time to remedy the situation.

MY TRUE HEALING ACTION PLAN

Who are three people in my life I can call true friends?

Starting today, what steps will I take to be a better friend and to have more friends?

18

ABOUT GIVING

WHY IS IT IMPORTANT THAT WE GIVE TO OTHERS? BECAUSE giving from the heart is "being alive with a faith that is put into action."

Grandma taught me that when we give, it is a demonstration of gratitude for what God has done for us. When we share what we have, from the heart, we will in turn receive what we need. Each time we give, we are professing our faith that regardless of how little we have, we believe in a world of plenty.

Growing up in Haiti, we did not have a lot, especially when Father was not around. But somehow, Grandma always managed to put aside something for the church and for the poor.

"You give because you should, not because you want people to know how nice you are," was her philosophy. "There is no more powerful instance than to know that your help can change someone's life."

I will never forget one time when Grandma and I visited the open market. I was about nine, talking about all the things I wanted Grandma to buy for me. She told me that money was scarce. Father worked for the government, and sometimes, as many as three months passed between his paychecks. That day, she only had five dollars to spend, only enough to buy the barest of necessities.

On the way to the market, a very distraught woman begged us to give her some change. She said one of her children was very sick, and she could not afford to buy medicine. Without hesitation, Grandma gave the woman a dollar. There were so many things we could have gotten with that dollar. Although Grandma knew that sometimes people lied to get money, she said we had to give anyway because the woman may really need the money to care for a sick child.

Grandma taught me that it's not necessary to know a person before you help them. Do not give merely to hear, "Oh, what a nice person you are." You give because you want to give, never expecting anything in return. It is not how much you have, but how much you have to share with others that matters.

I also learned that we have to be careful about how we give. Sometimes, by giving too much, such as to our children, we deprive them of learning the value of money.

But giving involves so much more than money. Showing compassion and caring or just a smile can make a difference in the lives of those who are suffering.

Sometimes, a small gift of time or energy at the right moment can make a world of difference. I remember telling my friend Sheri about the lack of electricity at the hospital in La Vallée de Jacmel, Haiti. When I performed procedures at that hospital, someone would have to hold a flashlight so I could see. The day before I left for Haiti, Sheri called to say she had a special gift for the women of La Vallée. Her husband Bob had designed and constructed an adjustable headlamp for me. What a blessed gift!

When we give, we show that we have faith in God and in humanity.

"The more I give, the more I have."

Louise Hay

"For as the body without the spirit is dead, so faith without works is dead also."

James 2:26

MY TRUE HEALING ACTION PLAN

Is giving part of my life?

Starting today, what steps will I take to share more financial help or to give more of my time?

19

BEING GRATEFUL

———

BE GRATEFUL FOR EVERYTHING THAT HAPPENS TO YOU, POSITIVE or negative, because every one of these experiences has taught you something.

You are less prone to be unhappy when you focus on things you're grateful for. You are more likely to be optimistic and feel good about yourself and to share your blessings.

Have you ever made a "Grateful List?" Please do so. You simply write down all that you are grateful for. In times of doubt or sadness, read your list, and add to it often.

As an example, here is my grateful list:

- Being healthy
- Having many true friends
- My siblings and other relatives
- Grandma, who came into my life to teach me beautiful lessons about faith
- Enjoying all the different kinds of work I do and hobbies I have
- Those who support my foundation and make it possible to help the children of Haiti

- Being optimistic and finding the best in everything and everyone
- Being able to judge all beings by their character and not their skin color, their material possessions, their sexual orientation, or their religion
- Having been given many unusual opportunities in my lifetime
- That special look in the eyes of a mother in La Vallée whose daughter I healed
- The wonderful feeling I have after returning from a medical mission in Haiti or from the clinic here in San Diego
- Being okay with my reflection in the mirror
- Knowing I have learned to take life one day at a time
- My beautiful garden with flowers, fruit, and birds playing
- Recognizing my good fortune to live in America
- Being able to leave the world a better place with my skills and caring

Upon awakening every morning, I take a deep breath and think about what I'm grateful for.

I believe that gratitude is an act of faith that allows us to remember where we come from, appreciate what we have, and share our blessings.

MY TRUE HEALING ACTION PLAN

What am I grateful for?

*Starting today, what steps will I take to create a Grateful List,
and how will I use it?*

20

KEEPING FAITH THROUGH ADVERSITIES

———ᗡᗡᗡ———

THE MAJORITY OF MY PATIENTS WHOSE HEALTH DETERIORATES IN spite of the best Western medical and alternative care available are those who lose their faith.

People who improve continue to have faith in a higher power even though they may have a chronic, painful condition or there's the possibility they may die. Their quality of life and ability to endure the discomfort caused by their illness and treatments are greatly enhanced by their faith.

Janet was diagnosed with scoliosis as a teen, and as long as she could remember, she always had pain in her upper and lower back. The pain was so severe that at the age of twenty-one, she had a stainless steel rod placed along her spine, secured by hooks attached to her vertebrae. Following that surgery, she was bedridden for a long time.

But Janet did well because she used her faith and prayers to help get her through the pain, surgery, and recovery. Years later she is thriving and has joined a support group on Facebook to share her experience and to help others.

My sister Fifi was diagnosed with breast cancer in 2000 and underwent a painful bilateral mastectomy and reconstruction. Following her recuperation, she continued to attend church, exercised regularly, ate mostly organic food, took time off for vacation, and travelled as much as she could afford.

Unfortunately, in September 2014 she was diagnosed with metastatic cancer that had spread to her lungs and around her heart and major blood vessels. She was fifty-nine years old. Soon, she started having difficulty breathing and walking and had to quit work.

When Fifi realized she was on the verge of dying, she decided she was going to live and prayed to do so. Her "why" reason was that she wanted to hold a baby granddaughter in her arms someday. She had two grown boys who were not at all interested in having babies yet, so she had to be healthy for few years to come.

Fifi had the "faith of the mustard seed" and had no doubt that her prayers were going to be answered. The family agreed that when we thought of her, we would see her already healed. She also had faith in me, her "angel," as she called me. We spent much time together, and as we prayed, we both visualized everything gone in her chest.

Her prayers sustained her through the horrible side effects of chemotherapy and radiation therapy, as she kept on visualizing holding her granddaughter. And verified by all her doctors, Fifi is now completely free of cancer.

""Commit your way to the Lord; Trust also in Him,
And He shall bring it to pass."

Psalm 37:5

"The harsher the situation, the harder you pray!"

Mary Thigpen AKA Sitting Owl

MY TRUE HEALING ACTION PLAN

When does my faith waver?

Starting today, what steps will I take to strengthen my faith?

21

SURROUND YOURSELF WITH THOSE WHO WALK IN FAITH

REGARDLESS OF THE STRENGTH OF YOUR FAITH, SOMETIMES, IT will falter. You might question it when bad things happen, or you might even turn your back on God. Hence, the importance of having people in your life who have unwavering faith and with whom you can rekindle your spirit and regain or renew your faith.

Oliver Wendell Holmes said:

> *"Trouble makes us one with every human being in the world—and unless we touch others, we're out of touch with life."*

Many people have been pillars throughout my personal spiritual journey, especially during the difficult time when I transformed from a Western, allopathic OB-GYN to an intuitive and spiritual healer. Several people I know made a profound impact on me with their faith, and I would like to share their stories with you...

TRUE STORIES OF AMAZING PEOPLE WHO INSPIRED ME TO CHERISH MY FAITH

Guy Moreau

It was November 1999, a month after my mother's death, and four months after I quit surgery and decided to join a friend to provide free medical services in Haiti. Guy, my brother-in-law, was standing by his stalled car on the Palmetto Expressway in Florida when a vehicle hit him and burst into flames, trapping him under it. At great risk, strangers who saw the accident lifted the car and pulled him out. He was airlifted unconscious to the burn unit at Jackson Memorial Hospital. The right side of his head, face, neck, arm, hand, fingers, and upper chest were severely burned. They had to amputate the fingers of his right hand and perform multiple surgeries to save his right arm. Doctors weren't sure if he would be blind.

Guy, who had been a handsome man, was now skin and bones and badly disfigured. At first, we thought he had sustained brain damage, since despite his severe injuries he always greeted us with a smile and never complained. But Guy was aware of everything that had happened. He told me and the rest of the family not to worry; he was going to be okay. Other people he met during his physical therapy sessions were not as fortunate in his eyes: they were blind, paraplegic, quadriplegic, unable to speak, or worse. He said he believed in God and looked forward to learning the reason his life had been spared.

On New Year's Eve, Guy and I sat together in his hospital room. The television was on. A commercial aired, featuring Christopher Reeve who played superman but at the age of forty-two was involved in an equestrian accident that made him a quadriplegic, kept alive by a breathing machine.

"See!" Guy said, "He's accepted what happened to him. So do I." He also told me that since he loved his wife, my sister Fifi, too much to let her see him suffering, he decided he would just have to be strong enough for the both of them.

Guy went home on February 11 and on February 14 he sent me an e-mail that said: *May the beauty of this day bring you love and joy!*

The miracle of my bother-in-law's survival and his amazing attitude inspired and encouraged me. While he still required more surgeries and rehabilitation for disfiguring burn injuries, Guy's faith remained strong for my sister Fifi as she battled breast cancer a few months later. He was not only strong for her; he remained strong for all of us. He comforted us and gave each of us strength, in spite of his personal tragedies. I realized then that this was why his life had been spared, so he could be a spiritual pillar for our family.

Sheri Thurman

My life was in turmoil as I tried to make it as a Western doctor, and my body responded with severe heartburn that persisted, in spite of watching my diet and taking antacids and heartburn medications. Before I left for Haiti, a patient of mine, Sheri, called and asked me to their house, saying she had a donation for me; her husband Bob, a firefighter, had developed a headlamp to use when I did medical procedures in Haiti with no electricity.

When I arrived at her home, she offered me lemonade, but I declined, saying I suffered from heartburn that would not respond to treatment.

"If you let me," Sheri said, "I can lay my hand on your stomach and ask Jesus to heal you, and he will."

It was an awkward situation, a patient laying hands on her medical doctor and asking God to heal her.

The moment made me recall how Sheri had reacted when she came to my office right after Guy had been badly burned and was fighting for his life in the intensive care burn unit. Sheri was also a burn victim; when she was four years old and playing with matches, her dress caught on fire. She suffered extensive, third-degree burns and had multiple hospitalizations and surgeries into her late teens.

"Oh, my," she had said, upon hearing about Guy, "The Lord told me this morning that you needed a miracle before Christmas."

Then she held my hand and prayed I would be accorded that miracle— that Guy would survive his injuries. And he did because of his will to live, his faith, and the prayers of so many people of faith like Sheri.

I agreed to let Sheri summon her husband, their son Kenny, and their grandson Nickolus, and we made a circle in the middle of her living room. She laid her left hand on my stomach and raised her right hand.

Kenny was touching her at the elbow with his right hand while holding Nickolus' right hand; Nickolus had his left hand touching my right knee. Sheri started to pray.

I have nothing to lose, I thought. Grandma was dead, but for the moment she'd been replaced by Sheri, who was laying hands on me and praying to heal my uncontrollable heartburn. As I did when Grandma would touch me and pray for me, I opened myself to healing. Sheri's prayers worked. I no longer have chronic heartburn.

Sheri and her husband are angels who support my Angels for Haiti Project. When I visit, we always end with a prayer, and I always leave them feeling spiritually uplifted.

Edna Parish

One time when my mother came to visit me in San Diego, I introduced her to Edna Parish, with whom I had a special friendship. She asked Edna to please take good care of me. Edna took those words to heart, calling me "Sis" and "my Georgia peach."

Edna would call me and invite me over to eat delicious, Louisiana food. Many of my books and writings were conceived on scraps of paper at her kitchen table. When projects I started outside of my medical practice would fail to bring me financial relief, I would go to her, sit in her kitchen, and cry my heart out.

Seated next to me she would hold my face with both hands and say, "My Georgia peach, you have to trust that the Lord loves you, and all that is happening in your life is for your own good. You can ask whatever you want, but only he knows what's best for you. And one day, when it's least expected, it will come, like a shower of rain."

Edna's faith was unwavering and inspires me to this day.

Godfroy Boursiquot

In 2003, I met Godfroy Boursiquot, aka "Gody," a warm, engaging person, a philosopher, and a serious thinker about education. He was born in Tuff, in La Vallée de Jacmel, Haiti and eventually moved to Port-au-Prince, where he started to teach children who lived in the streets and the cemeteries. He earned a degree in communication and journalism with an emphasis on children's rights. Because of his activism, at the age of twenty-two, he had to go into hiding and went deep into the woods for two months in order to save his life. That episode only reinforced his commitment. He then wrote an educational program that included a sustainability plan for both children and adults in any community—wherever the person was living. A year later, he created one of the first Haitian, non-governmental organizations—NGO CODEHA, or *Corde Enfants Haitiens*—to disseminate this revolutionary approach. He was a guest speaker at many U.S. universities, including Harvard, spoke at the UN for children's rights, worked for foreign NGOs such as UNICEF, and served as mediator for armed children in the streets to surrender during conflicts. He eventually worked with community members to build a community center and educational compound in his home town in Haiti.

Due to political insecurities, Gody had to immigrate with his family to the U.S. in 2007. But he continued to go back home to work as often as funds permitted. His perseverance and faith inspired many.

Together, we have worked on many programs to best serve our children in La Vallée. Over the years, Gody put much energy into building the CODEHA compound that serves as a community center and trade school in Tuff. In an area with over ninety-five percent unemployment, the only hope for our youth is to have a trade as well as the opportunity to learn how to be an entrepreneur. Unfortunately, the compound was badly damaged by the devastating earthquake that struck Haiti in January 2010 and had to be condemned.

As we tried very hard to find funds to repair the compound, I would become discouraged. But Gody always remained positive. He reminded me that when we're confronted with obstacles, we have to believe we're on the right track and continue no matter what.

Gody is the epitome of optimism, trust, and faith.

Reverend Joy Almaas

Although I've sung in choirs since childhood, in April 2015, I felt inspired to take singing lessons and found a good voice teacher. After my first lesson, I was in a store when a woman approached me, saying she knew me from somewhere.

"You're Rosie," I said. "We both belonged to a church choir in 2003, which I left when I got very busy. Would you believe that for some crazy reason, I just decided to take voice lessons and had my first one today?"

"Perfect," she replied. "You should join us again."

So I did and even had the privilege of having the choir director, Reverend Joy Almaas, pick me up and drop me home each time we practiced or performed.

Little did I know that rejoining the choir was going to help me spiritually. Not only did I gain a new family with the choir members, but I also added joy to my life by learning spiritual songs and singing in front of the congregation. The other bonus was the one-on-one time spent with Reverend Joy, driving back and forth to the church. She is a great spiritual teacher, and receiving her words of wisdom and encouragement helped me to better understand myself as a spiritual healer, even to the extent of healing myself...

During the largest fire recorded in California history, called the "Fire Siege of 2003," I suffered severe smoke inhalation and had to evacuate to Los Angeles to a friend's house, where I stayed for two weeks. The fire started on October 26, 2003 and was finally contained on November 3, having caused the worst damage in the history of San Diego County and California. It burned over two hundred eighty thousand acres, two thousand two hundred and thirty-two homes—and killed fifteen people, including one firefighter; many more people were severely hurt.

Since then, whenever I would come in contact with polluted air, my sensitive lungs got something like an asthma attack, and my bronchus would constrict, I had difficulty breathing and coughing spells. It dismayed me that smoke damage restricted my ability to go places and that I had to carry an inhaler.

As we drove to choir practice, I discussed this condition with Reverend Joy. She encouraged me to say out loud that it was my intention that my lungs were going to be healed. She helped me remember that I have helped so many patients heal over the years, patients who, according to the scientific world, could not be healed, and that I could and should do the same for myself.

If you go with your spiritual self, your intuition, and the inheritance from your Grandma and Grand Père, requesting that the spirit moves through you, I told myself, you can heal yourself. I thought this and said this over and over, and it worked. Now I don't even remember where my inhaler is.

Reverend Joy also taught me to say the following prayer when I feel overwhelmed: "Father, Mother, Life, you are my life, my constant support, my health, my protection, my perfect fulfillment of every need and my highest inspiration. Father, Mother, Life, thy will be done in this situation. This looks like a shitty broken mess to me. Please take it, and fix it for me. Show me a better way." I also use this one each time I help a patient: "I of myself do nothing, but the spirit within me does the work."

Being in the choir and being influenced in such a positive way by Reverend Joy's faith encouraged me to continue with my spiritual journey, enabling me to be even more helpful to my patients.

Mary Thigpen, AKA Sitting Owl

I turned my home into a healing center in 2005. Since I am a gynecologist and my experience was limited to women, I was troubled that I didn't feel comfortable seeing male patients. My long-time friend Mary Thigpen certainly changed that.

Mary and her husband Dr. Willie Thigpen, a family practitioner in San Diego, were both from New Orleans. I called Mary an angel who touched many lives. She had the sensitivity to *know* when someone was going through a rough time. Invariably, when I was feeling sad, I'd get a call from Mary, inviting me out someplace or over to share her husband's famous New Orleans gumbo.

When she found out I had been using my healing touch to help women in distress, she was elated. Mary brought a stream of friends—women *and men*—"who needed just to sit in the garden and have a little laying of hands in front of the waterfall." Sometimes, I would get a call from her to go and pray for a sick friend in the hospital. She called me her prayer warrior. I never asked any questions and would accommodate Mary and her friends, women and men, the best I could.

In August 2005, Hurricane Katrina hit the Gulf of Mexico, sweeping through Texas, Louisiana, Mississippi, Alabama, and Florida. New

Orleans, built below sea level, suffered the worst damage, as flooding waters flew over or through shattered levees. There were over one thousand three hundred deaths and many people unaccounted for. Over ninety percent of the residents of southeast Louisiana were evacuated. Unfortunately, many elderly and poor remained. The Louisiana Superdome was used as a shelter for more than fourteen thousand people. As the world watched the tragedy unfold, as with most people, I felt powerless.

Mary's family and in-laws were among those affected. As Mary went back and forth to help rebuild shattered lives, I shared with her how I wished I could do something for the victims. Then I got an exciting phone call from her in the beginning of June 2008.

"Carolle," she said. "My brother Bobby Lorell Johnson is the founder of a non-profit organization called Family Advocacy & Neighborhood Services—FANS—that has been helping New Orleans elderly populations, as well as youth who were impacted by Hurricane Katrina. His organization is having a luncheon, where eight hundred and fifty seniors will have the opportunity to mingle with celebrities, eat good food, and be entertained by the best New Orleans has to offer. Pease tell me you are available from June 12-15; you will have the opportunity to lay hands on as many seniors as you can that day. And, yes, I will get your plane ticket...No, no, no...it's on me."

Of course, I went. I drove through parish after parish in New Orleans, and my heart was breaking, as I saw ghost towns and homes with distinct high-water marks caused by them being under water for months. I saw the infamous trailers and people still living in them in the blistering heat and humidity.

We entered a huge, nicely decorated ballroom; a Zydeco band played lively music on the main stage. Rectangular tables stood along the walls, upon which sat gifts to be raffled off for the attendees. Seniors of all racial backgrounds, wearing colorful attire, sat quietly at round tables for twelve. On one side of the room were tables full of Creole cuisine that filled the air with flavorful aromas.

When it was my turn to speak, I was introduced by the MC as "Angel Dr. Carolle" who was going to provide hands-on healing for stress relief to those who wanted it. I thanked Mary and her brother Bobby for giving me such an opportunity to be of service. I explained that the healing touch consisted of standing behind them and touching their forehead, temples, scalp, and sometimes, their upper back, as the spirit guided me. They could choose to close their eyes. The touch usually lasted less than a minute.

As I got down from the podium, one elderly woman in a wheelchair raised her hand, and I went to her. When she opened her eyes again, those seated near may have sensed something because they quickly raised their hands, too. I then went from table to table, touching all who raised their hands. Beforehand, I had asked for help from God, the Holy Spirit, and the love that had been stored from all over the world from those who felt helpless and wanted to give to those who were suffering. I never grew tired.

That day, I touched about one hundred and twenty-five seniors and volunteers; it was like going through a intensive residency training, where I learned how to refine my healing touch techniques. Little did I know this experience was going to serve me well when I would go to Haiti following the devastating earthquake in January 2010. Mary's Thigpen's faith in me enhanced my own faith, and the faith of those who benefited from my healing touch.

It is never too late to find spiritual role models to strengthen your faith.

"Imitate those who through faith and patience inherit the promises."

Hebrews 6:12

"Surround yourself only with people who will take you higher."

Oprah Winfrey

MY TRUE HEALING ACTION PLAN

Do I have people in my life who walk in faith?

Starting today, what steps will I take to find those people?

22

BUILDING FAITH BY READING

THROUGHOUT HISTORY, PEOPLE HAVE KNOWN THAT SPIRITUAL reading offers great benefits to their souls. One of the most read books in the history of mankind is the Bible, which can be read alone, at church through scriptures, and at Bible studies.

Those who believe, pray, and read scriptures are less likely to be plagued with mental and physical illnesses and are better able to cope with health problems. Grandma, even though she could barely read, would not go a day without reading her prayer books and singing hymns out loud. The harsher life was for her, the more time she spent praying, singing, and reading.

Reading inspirational books by spiritual people and applying the information to your life, especially during hard times, can be extremely helpful. And now in the age of the Internet and smartphones, it's even easier to access helpful books, poems, articles, and blogs. Reading and practicing what you read will only augment your ability to grow spiritually, enriching your faith.

Not long after talking with a friend, Yves Domond, about my sister's cancer he sent me a beautiful, handmade greeting card by Faith Saunders, a personal growth coach, writer, artist, and the founder of "Discover a New Future." The card pictured a pot with flowers and hovering butterflies. The front simply read: *You are not alone.* Inside was the poem *Footprints in the Sand*, written by Mary Stevenson in 1936 and copyrighted by her in 1984 from her original text. Reading the beautiful words, I felt moved, and my faith was rejuvenated. Here it is, for when *you* need it...

FOOTPRINTS IN THE SAND

One night I dreamed I was walking along the beach with the Lord.

Many scenes from my life flashed across the sky.

In each scene I noticed footprints in the sand.

Sometimes there were two sets of footprints,

Other times there were one set of footprints.

This bothered me because I notice that during the low periods of my life,

When I was suffering from anguish, sorrow or defeat,

I could see only one set of footprints.

So I said to the Lord,

"You promised me Lord, that if I followed you, you would walk with me always.

But I have noticed that during the most trying periods of my life

There have only been one set of footprints in the sand.

Why, when I needed you most, you have not been there for me?"

The Lord replied,

"The times when you have seen only one set of footprints,

Is when I carried you."

MY TRUE HEALING ACTION PLAN

How would spiritual reading benefit me?

Starting today, what steps will I take to read more?

23

THE POWER OF PRAYERS

─···─

MANY PEOPLE FIND ANSWERS TO LIFE'S TRAGEDIES IN PRAYER.
Studies have documented lower rates of depression and anxiety-
related illness among those who pray. Other studies have
demonstrated better outcomes among patients who were prayed for,
as compared to patients who were not.

Prayers are known to bring relaxation, hope, and comfort. A belief in
what you are praying for is very important. I pray for my patients who
are undergoing chemotherapy. When someone I know is going to have
a life-threatening surgery, I always ask for the date and exact time
when the surgery will take place, and I pray during those times.
Growing up in Haiti, living through many heart-wrenching situations, I
believe I survived and helped others heal because of prayer.

Grandma prayed at least an hour every day. Even though I did not pray
for myself during my rebellious years in Haiti, I always depended on
her to pray for me. While I was doing obstetrics, whenever a
premature baby was in neonatal intensive care, Grandma and I both
prayed for the baby. The babies always did very well, regardless of
how premature they were. One of them, Megan, was two pounds when
she was born. Her mother told me that knowing Grandma was praying
gave her hope that her daughter was going to survive. Megan did,
indeed, and is now a thriving young woman.

As the years went by, patients themselves began asking me to pray for them and with them. And when we do, I can see the transformation in their being occur in front of my eyes.

Each time I return to Haiti, I see my people living in extreme poverty, working in harsh environments. But Haitians are always hopeful that tomorrow will be a better day and that God will provide for them. They live simple lives, and they pray with great hope, even during times when their most basic needs are unmet. They are grateful for the small things; they thank God for what they have and do not complain about things they don't have.

While working at our small hospital with little means, I pray with patients before I touch them, giving them the opportunity to manifest their faith and heal themselves.

Going to Sunday Mass at St. John Baptist Church, the Saint Patron of La Vallée de Jacmel, where the prayers and singing are done in Haitian Kréyol and French makes me feel closer to God, Grandma, and Mother. I return to the U.S. feeling spiritually stronger.

I realize some people who pray constantly utter the words as a mechanical repetition without much or any meaning. I've had many patients who swear by the Bible or use a cross as a pendant while they still hold grudges and make everyone miserable around them, and they still suffer from their ills. To awaken them, I have them repeat a psalm or the Lord's Prayer with me, with intention and focus, and I watch for them to finally make sense of the words they've been uttering over and over. Only then can they heal themselves.

Once I had a patient who was holding on tight to past grudges and could not move forward in her life. I explained to her how I have taught my patients to pray and how they were able to strengthen their faith and heal themselves. I told her about Grandma's favorite prayer to the Sacred Heart of Jesus that I often use.

"But I'm Jewish," she said. "When I go to the synagogue, we pray to God."

"Is there a prayer we could use to pray together?" I asked.

"I don't have such a prayer," she said.

"You continue to go to the synagogue," I replied, "there has to be something there—some bit of scripture you use to help you to keep going."

"Well, there's the *Adon Olam* 'Lord of the World'. It's the final prayer of the *Musaf* service on *Shabbat* morning and festivals; it's also a bedtime prayer and is recited on one's deathbed. *'B'yado afkid ruchi be'eit'shan v'aira v'im ruchi gevi-a-ti Adonai li v'lo ira.'* 'Into God's hands I entrust my spirit, when I sleep and when I wake: and with my spirit and my body also, as long as God is with me I shall not fear.' Whenever they sing that song, I feel warmth in my heart."

"Why don't we just say the last verse *'Adonai li v'lo ira*—God is with me, I shall not fear.'?"

As she kneeled in front of me, I firmly held her hands in mine, looked into her beautiful green eyes, and together we prayed.

"Adonai li v'lo ira... Adonai li v'lo ira... Adonai li v'lo ira... Adonai li v'lo ira..."

There are many prayers that comfort me, especially this one below by Francis of Assisi. We live in a chaotic world, where there is so much suffering. If we could all live by these words of faith, the world would be a much better place.

Lord, make me an instrument of your peace.
Where there is hatred, let me sow love.
Where there is injury, pardon.
Where there is doubt, faith.
Where there is despair, hope.
Where there is darkness, light.
And where there is sadness, joy.
O Divine Master,
Grant me that I may not so much seek
To be consoled as to console,
To be understood as to understand,
To be loved as to love.
For it is in giving that we receive.
It is in pardoning that we are pardoned,
And in dying that we are born into eternal life.

"And all things, whatsoever ye shall ask in prayer, believing, ye shall receive."

Matthew 21:22

"Pray unceasingly! For our prayers to be heard by God, we must pray in faith and with humility and sincerity."

Mark 11:24

"Be anxious for nothing; but in everything by prayer and supplication with thanksgiving let your requests be made known unto God."

Philippians 4:6-8

"In God I trust and am not afraid. What can man do to me?"

Psalm 56:11

MY TRUE HEALING ACTION PLAN

What are my favorite prayers?

Starting today, what steps will I take to use prayers in my life more often?

24

THE POWER OF SURRENDER

———

SURRENDER INVOLVES LETTING GO OF YOUR EGO. SURRENDER happens after you gain understanding and belief that the Infinite is taking care of you, completely and totally, and that your ego should get out of the way of a higher wisdom.

A great number of my patients plagued with emotional and physical complaints are churchgoers, very active in their church community, and they proclaim deep religious faith.

Often, all their medical lab work is normal, they eat "healthy" diets made up of organic foods, work out at the gym or have a regular exercise routine, take vitamins, supplements, drink special water, etc., and yet, they aren't healthy.

Do you know what they invariably have in common? In spite of their strong faith, they do not surrender, which causes them to continue to be stressed, anxious, depressed, and feeling ill.

Doctors and medicines can help you with diseases and injuries. True healing, however, comes from within you, it's faith in action, and it requires surrendering to a power greater than yourself.

When I told my brother-in-law Guy—who kept a positive attitude following horrific burns, multiple surgeries, and chronic pain—that I wished I had his strength and faith, he said, "It's not merely strength or even faith; you *have to let go!*"

In her book *The Ecstasy of Surrender: 12 Surprising Ways Letting Go Can Empower Your Life*, Judith Orloff, MD explains,

> *"I'm intrigued with the idea of surrender, not as defeat or loss but as a positive, intuitive way of living, power that grows as you develop trust in the moment as well as in change and the unknown.*
>
> *Learning when to let go versus when to assert control is the secret formula to vibrant health, longevity, wellness, healing, success, pleasure, and happiness."*

There are endless examples of my patients who were soon able to enjoy renewed health when they finally realized the correlation between the symptoms they were suffering and their feelings of not being in control and being distraught over difficult situations.

I would remind them to leave it to God, pray when they would feel overwhelmed, and sometimes have a good cry to release the angst and toxins accumulated in their bodies. They had to learn how to keep faith and see that when they surrender, help will come.

After having to fend for myself for as long as I could remember, I used to have difficulty surrendering. The panic attacks I suffered were a true blessing to me; they made me realize I was in control of nothing. Now, the quicker I surrender the better for me. By knowing when to let go of control, I've improved my life: I am able to live in the moment, knowing the future will always take care of itself.

When things do not happen the way we hoped, it means we are supposed to learn about the patience required to surrender to faith.

I have a wonderful prayer next to my computer, where I spend a great deal of time writing. Whenever I feel the uncertainty of life starting to create havoc, I read it, and I feel better.

Here it is, plus additional helpful thoughts:

"May today there be peace within.

May you trust that you are exactly where you are meant to be.

May you not forget the infinite possibilities that are born of faith in yourself and others.

May you use the gifts that you have received, and pass on the love that has been given to you.

May you be content with yourself just the way you are.

Let this knowledge settle into your bones, and allow your soul the freedom to sing, dance, praise, and love. It is there for each and every one of us."

Sainte Thérèse de Lisieux

"Look at the birds of the air; they neither sow nor reap nor gather into barns, and yet your heavenly Father keeps feeding them. Are you not worth much more than they?"

Matthew 6:26

"Even when we can't understand why certain things happen, we must trust that it is what it is and that all is as it's meant to be.

Some lessons are best learned through pain.

Sometimes, our visions clear only after our eyes are washed with tears.

Sometimes, we have to be broken so we can be whole again.

Remember: If God made the day to be perfect, He wouldn't have invented tomorrow."

Kirvy

MY TRUE HEALING ACTION PLAN

What do I know about surrendering my ego and control?

Starting today, what steps will I take to learn how to surrender?

25

BEING PART OF A RELIGIOUS
OR SPIRITUAL COMMUNITY

─᯾᯾─

IT IS ESTIMATED THAT A PERSON IN THE UNITED STATES CAN expect to move *11.7 times* in their lifetime, thwarting the opportunity to form deep bonds and solid friendships. This often results in chronic loneliness, depression, and even addiction.

One of the most basic human needs is the need for community. Science has shown that being part of a spiritual community gives people the opportunity to belong and the ability to develop and share spiritually in a supportive environment. During good times, having someone with whom you can share experiences and accomplishments enhances the fun and creates fond memories. During hard times, knowing there are trustworthy, caring people to turn to for a listening ear and guidance is an essential asset to well-being.

According to research, those who participate in church functions benefit more than those who pray alone. Members of a spiritual community enjoy a reciprocal arrangement due to their participation in the community and the social support they receive in return. There are dozens of ways belonging to a spiritual or religious community can enrich your life. Some of these are reading scriptures/attending bible studies, doing worthwhile projects together such as fundraising, helping those in need—visiting the sick in their home or in the hospital, taking someone a warm meal, assisting those who have no loved ones around—and assisting at functions in the church—working as an usher, participating in Sunday school, volunteering to lead youth programs or chaperone a field trip. Your spiritual growth will benefit from the wisdom of those more experienced and will be enhanced by the synergy of others working together for a common goal.

If you already belong to a church, ask yourself how you could get more involved. The more you give, the more you will receive. Being of service to those in need is uplifting and a diversion from your own difficulties. Attend a prayer service; research has shown that regular prayers, scripture readings, and bible study provide health benefits. Being with spiritually minded people dedicated to deepening their relationship with God is inspiring and exhilarating.

It has been my experience that those who continue to worship in the faith of their childhood have greater health benefits and quality of life than those who are "recovered" Christian, Jews, or other religions who now consider themselves "spiritual," implying they are freed from unnecessary dogma. You may be like many who were turned off by religions because of dogma and creed or were part of a religion that does not portray God as merciful and benevolent.

If you have not become a part of a religious community and are inclined to do so, especially if you are new to an area, you may want to visit as many different churches and religious groups as you want until you find one that has a belief system similar to yours and where you feel you belong. If you have children, a gift you can give to them is to be part of such a community.

"Whether we are in a mosque, church, or synagogue, we are talking to God in every language that he understands. We are using hymns and liturgy, and I know we are getting through to the same God."

Rudy Giuliani, former mayor of NYC

MY TRUE HEALING ACTION PLAN

Do I belong to a community that supports my spirit and strengthens my faith?

Starting today, what steps will I take to find that community?

Concluding Thoughts

PLEASE DO NOT FORGET; WE ARE ALL ON A SPIRITUAL JOURNEY.

To me, admitting you have a soul and then taking care of it leads to spiritual health. How do you take care of it? Find whatever you call a higher power, and lay your ego at its feet. This will free your soul and allow you to have faith and trust in something bigger than yourself. It will give you a broader perspective on life and the lessons we are here to learn.

Having faith, as well as learning how to take care of yourself, having healthy boundaries in all areas of your life, practicing forgiveness, giving from your heart, and having a connection with nature will lighten your stress, your sorrows, and your heart.

Put some time aside each day to pray, read a good book, or study your favorite scripture. These days, family members do not spend time together and are separated by TV, computers, video games, smartphones, and social media. When possible, pray with family members. It has been proven to be beneficial for all involved. Family members who pray together tend to communicate with each other better and have the ability to resolve small issues before they take on a life of their own.

Be grateful for everything that happens to you because these experiences, good or bad, happen for a reason and teach you something. Upon awaking every morning, give thanks for being alive. This planet is a huge schoolroom—anything that happens can be transformed into something positive by your spiritual beliefs, thoughts, and deeds.

Know deep in your heart that you will be taken care of, no matter what.

I no longer fret about what should or should not be happening. I know that all things unfold in divine order, that adversities are lessons I am supposed to learn for my own good, and you do not always get what you ask for when you ask for it.

That morning in November 2014 when I awoke totally healed after surrendering control and asking God for help has really deepened my faith. I truly know in my heart that regardless of the adversity, *with faith I will overcome it.*

My hope is that, after reading this book, you will understand that for yourself, as well— that you will be taken care of, always, no matter what.

Believe, surrender, trust, and always have faith.

ACKNOWLEDGMENTS

THANK YOU TO GRANDMA AND ALL MY FAMILY, FRIENDS, patients, and mentors, and thank you to Karen Wilkening, my keen editor who brainstorms with me and refines the material.

About the Author

DR. CAROLLE JEAN-MURAT, MD IS A GIFTED INTUITIVE AND spiritual healer, trained as a board-certified obstetrician and gynecologist and primary care specialist who has helped thousands of men and women over the past four decades.

Born in 1950 and raised in Haiti, she comes from a family of healers, shamans, herbalists, and midwives. Dr. Carolle was educated in top universities in Haiti, Mexico, Jamaica, and the U.S., giving her a broad-spectrum approach to medicine and invaluable multicultural knowledge. She has worked with under-privileged patients in dire conditions, even performing surgeries by flashlight in Haiti. She has also practiced medicine in highly acclaimed, technologically advanced hospitals in the U.S., helping thousands of men and women, including wounded warriors suffering from post-traumatic stress disorder (PTSD) and military sexual trauma (MST).

Dr. Carolle is a Fellow of the American Congress of Obstetricians and Gynecologists. She had a successful private practice in San Diego, California from 1982 to 2005. In 2005, she closed her private practice in San Diego because she could no longer fit into a prescription-writing, bottom-line-oriented medical system that did not allow time and resources for doctors to properly care for patients as whole human beings. She would not compromise.

Her dream was to continue treating and healing patients, using her own ideals. She created the *Dr. Carolle Wellness & Retreat Center of San Diego,* where those who were ill or suffering could spend as much time as they needed with her.

Fluent in five languages, Dr. Carolle combines her scientific knowledge with her extraordinary gift of intuition and clairvoyance to help those who are ready to heal. Her process helps to discover the root cause of patients' symptoms and teaches them how to use this information to begin the healing process. With faith and caring she guides patients and shows them their strengths, teaches them how to let go, and simultaneously helps them overcome the obstacles that have prevented them from being their best self.

Dr. Carolle has always felt strongly about serving others, especially the poor and underprivileged. For more than three decades, Dr. Carolle has provided free medical care to the people of Haiti and underserved clinics in San Diego through Catholic Charities, and as a volunteer in medical clinics in several countries. Her own non-profit charity, *Health Through Communication Foundation,* is focused on providing medical care, education, and other needed services to the people of Haiti and the world.

As an international motivational speaker, Dr. Carolle brings her message of self-empowerment and faith through her award-winning books, private retreats, workshops, blogs, and podcasts.

CONTACT DR. CAROLLE

drcarolle@drcarolle.com

www.DrCarolle.com

OTHER BOOK
BY DR. CAROLLE

—⌇—

FORGIVING YOURSELF & OTHERS: *How to unleash your future by freeing yourself from past traumas*

Unresolved childhood issues are one of the major causes of unhappiness and dis-ease. Learn how healing unloving or hurtful relationships with others and with ourselves is the most crucial step we can take in our lives.

www.drcarolle.com/store/

GET SPECIAL DEALS
ON MORE BEST SELLING BOOKS

Get discounts and special deals on our best selling books at

www.tckpublishing.com/bookdeals